# IDEAS & HOW-TO
# Trimwork

Meredith® Books
Des Moines, Iowa

# IDEAS & HOW-TO

# Trimwork

*Better Homes and Gardens® Ideas & How-To Trimwork*
Editor: Paula Marshall
Contributing Project Manager: Mindy Pantiel
Contributing Editors: Rebecca Jerdee, Cathy Long
Associate Design Director: Todd Emerson Hanson
Contributing Graphic Designer: David Jordan, Studio 22
Copy Chief: Terri Fredrickson
Copy Editor: Kevin Cox
Publishing Operations Manager: Karen Schirm
Senior Editor, Asset & Information Management: Phillip Morgan
Edit and Design Production Coordinator: Mary Lee Gavin
Editorial Assistant: Kaye Chabot
Book Production Managers: Pam Kvitne, Marjorie J. Schenkelberg, Rick von Holdt, Mark Weaver
Imaging Center Operator: Jill Reed
Contributing Copy Editor: Joyce Gemperlein
Contributing Proofreaders: Sue Fetters, Sherry Hames, Sara Henderson, Heidi Johnson
Cover Photographer: Jon Jensen
Contributing Photographer: Scott Little
Contributing Indexer: Stephanie Ryman, Indexing Solutions
Contributing Illustrator: Robert LaPointe

**Meredith® Books**
Editor in Chief: Gregory H. Kayko
Executive Director, Design: Matt Strelecki
Managing Editor: Amy Tincher-Durik
Executive Editor: Benjamin W. Allen
Senior Editor/Group Manager: Vicki Leigh Ingham
Senior Associate Design Director: Ken Carlson
Marketing Product Manager: Brent Wiersma

Editorial Director: Linda Raglan Cunningham
Executive Director, Marketing: Kevin Kacere
Executive Director, New Business Development: Todd M. Davis
Executive Director, Sales: Ken Zagor
Director, Operations: George A. Susral
Director, Production: Douglas M. Johnston
Director, Marketing & Publicity: Amy Nichols
Business Director: Jim Leonard

Vice President and General Manager: Douglas J. Guendel

*Better Homes and Gardens® Magazine*
Editor in Chief: Gayle Goodson Butler
Deputy Editor, Home Design: Oma Blaise Ford

**Meredith Publishing Group**
President: Jack Griffin
Senior Vice President: Karla Jeffries

**Meredith Corporation**
Chairman of the Board: William T. Kerr
President and Chief Executive Officer: Stephen M. Lacy

In Memoriam: E. T. Meredith III (1933–2003)

# ■ Contents

# ◼ Introduction

Decorative trimwork once was an integral part of home design. Architects considered trimwork and built-ins of so much significance that they were often included in the blueprints. These details help to distinguish one architectural style of house from another.

The postwar housing boom and the advent of the "builder" home drastically changed all that. As low-budget homes were built at an astonishing rate, with the exception of simple baseboards and window casings, interior architectural details all but disappeared. Many people grew up in houses not only devoid of these details, but lacking in visual personality.

You don't, however, have to continue living in uninteresting two-dimensional rooms. With the help of this book, you can devise plans for adding details—from simple chair rails and wainscoting, also called wainscot, to more complicated built-in cabinets and window seats. The three parts of this book are designed to take you from the basic to the more complex, with plenty of inspiring ideas and practical how-to suggestions throughout.

*Part I* begins with trim basics such as crown molding, baseboards and wall paneling and continues into slightly more demanding elements such as window and door designs and casings. The section concludes with the decorative and functional aspects of columns, which can make a neoclassic statement and are effective room dividers, and an array of ceiling treatment options.

*Part II* is titled "Making a Statement" because staircases, fireplaces, and built-in cabinetry and seating can make a major impact on a space. This section is filled with strategies for creating these beautiful and functional focal points.

Continuity is critical to successfully incorporating architectural details in any home. *Part III* begins with a series of case studies selected to show how well-planned trimwork themes can visually tie all the spaces in a home together. Also in this section do-it-yourselfers can pick up tips on tool selection and find instructions on the basic techniques required for many trimwork projects.

Trimwork has its own language, and the glossary at the end of this book is a trusted reference that will guide even the novice do-it-yourselfer through all the unique terms.

Look for sidebars and illustrations to enhance your understanding of trimwork vocabulary and to demonstrate how to accomplish selected trimwork tasks. Use this book as your guide to creating richly layered living spaces that say something about where you live.

# PART I

# Trim Basics

Trimwork can be as simple as a piece of crown molding added to accentuate a door frame or built up to add drama to the top of a wall. In a room that soars a wainscot panel topped with a chair rail brings the space down to human scale. Columns serve to divide rooms while pilasters break up wall spaces, and the way you trim your windows and doors can set the tone for your house.

# The Joy of

The emergence and popularity of trimwork has, as with all things involving style, ridden the ebbs and flows of consumer interest. Today, it is again emerging as an important architectural element in home design. You'll find contemporary applications of cornices, crown molding, and casings to suit all preferences.

# Trimwork

# ■ Why Use Trimwork?

The look of room after room of nothing but flat white walls is, well, boring. Without trimwork, all houses are pretty much the same—a series of unadorned interconnected boxes.

Crown molding and baseboards add to this ordinary design, just as the right frame brings a piece of artwork into focus. Trimwork similarly defines a living or dining room. Window and door casings have a similar effect on previously plain, non-distinctive openings.

Install a carved mantel on an uninspired family room fireplace and watch a two-dimensional woodburner transform into a three-dimensional focal point. Never underestimate the ability of beautifully crafted cabinetry, custom window seats, or well-placed bookcases to enhance the function and interior design of a space.

Trimwork has many names and covers a variety of elements—molding, plasterwork, and architectural details are among the most common—but whatever you call it, taking the time to learn how to enhance your home with such things as cornices, columns, arches, and beams will ultimately add to the style and appeal of your home.

Including architectural details in a home will not only result in a level of design sophistication that will enrich the day-to-day living experience, it also will add financial value.

## A VIEW OF A ROOM

The look of this beautifully detailed room was created using trim pieces available through most local home centers or lumberyards and is within the capabilities of most do-it-yourselfers. Painting the suite of trim all one color provides continuity and delicately frames the subtle wall color.

**1. Cornice** molding creates a decorative transition between wall and ceiling, and crown moldings are generally installed at an angle to the wall. Here they come together to create a deeper profile that draws attention to the far wall.

**2.** Continuing the heavy profile on the far wall all the way around the room would have made the space feel top-heavy. Instead, a lighter cornice strip continues the line.

**3.** Window **casings** give openings more importance.

**4. Pilasters**, decorative half-columns set directly against a wall that mimic full columns, provide additional visual interest.

**5.** A **chair rail** set at the same height as the furnishings and created with the same molding style used on the ceiling runs around the perimeter of the room.

**6.** For balance the **baseboard** that conceals any gaps between the wall and flooring is sized to complement the crown molding treatment above.

**7.** A painted fireplace **mantel** and **mantelshelf** project just far enough into the room to make a three-dimensional statement without overwhelming.

## UNDERSTANDING TRIM

The most common types of trim are the ones that instantly improve wall expanses—cornices, crowns, and baseboards. On a practical level they hide the less-than-perfect joints between walls and floors or ceilings. On a decorative level trim transforms spaces by affecting the perception of a room's shape and size. Slender cornice or crown molding profiles can create a strong line that draws the eye around the room, making it feel larger. Conversely, a thick, detailed molding profile can add visual weight to a soaring wall and make a room feel cozier (for more about the effects of trim, see Chapter 2: "Adding Detail").

When choosing new trim first think about the finish. Whether it will be painted, stained, or left natural determines the material selection. Wood is the traditional choice, but while its beauty is undeniable, it's not your only option. If you're planning to paint the trim, manufactured materials, such as medium-density fiberboard (MDF), are highly convincing stand-ins for wood and are usually less expensive.

If you plan to stain wood trim or simply seal it to preserve its natural beauty, the type of wood is critical. Grain is only one consideration; each variety of wood has an inherent color and a unique personality that impact decor and suitablity for different applications. For example, the highly textural, open grain of oak is still obvious even beneath a coat of paint, while the closed grain of pine or poplar makes for a smoother surface, painted or stained. Freshly milled cherry has a rich, reddish orange hue that darkens with age; unstained oak may be white or red and will grow only slightly deeper in color with time.

Maple, in hard and soft varieties, is prized for its pale golden tone. Pine also has a yellowish color, while poplar can take on a yellowish-green cast. Fir has a rich, mellow tone that falls somewhere between gold and amber. Select a wood color that complements the overall design palette.

Plastic molding, including urethanes and other synthetics, is a goodlooking, budget-conscious alternative. Ideal for the do-it-yourselfer, it is lightweight and easy to cut, won't warp or shrink, and is available at home centers. Designed to

This cottage living room gets its elegant look from readily available stock molding. The hefty-looking crown molding is actually two inexpensive pieces, and the baseboards are a plain length of medium-density fiberboard topped with a piece of trim. The salvaged fireplace mantel was cut to fit and painted to match the rest of the trimwork, including the new window casings.

resemble expensive plaster, these synthetic materials must be painted, or they will look like plastic. Very expensive and difficult to install, plaster trimwork is usually reserved for historical preservation situations or high-end home renovations.

## STOCK OR CUSTOM-MILLED?

Most standard or stock moldings are available at home centers and lumberyards and, when installed properly, produce pleasing results. However, stock profiles alone don't provide the full range of options: Single-piece moldings may be too small or too thin or don't accurately emulate a certain architectural period. The solution is often to combine single-piece moldings with custom-milled profiles to achieve a specific look. To design your own profile or match an existing one, try a custom woodworking shop, mail order outlet, or Internet site that caters to woodworkers. These are often reasonably priced and will yield the results you want.

# ■ What's Your Style?

When selecting trim and molding patterns your imagination is limitless, and the style you select will depend on the architecture of the house, the interior design, and personal taste. For example, in a Greek Revival structure that is fronted by a two-story portico with massive columns, classical trim selections for the interiors are the most suitable. Those who love period decorating may want to choose moldings that complement a certain time in history (see "A Lesson in History" sidebar, page 20).

The relatively unadorned modern interiors typical of builder homes lend themselves to the blending of styles; the eclectic look is wonderful as long as the styles selected are not totally unrelated.

Peruse the examples here to gain a basic understanding of common styles.

**GREEK REVIVAL**

Do you gravitate toward the clean and simple? Then consider classical elements like fluted columns, extra tall windows, and subtle ceiling trim—all hallmarks of Greek Revival.

## GEORGIAN REVIVAL

If you favor highly symmetrical spaces, ceiling moldings with strong linear patterns and bold cornices then you are in the Georgian camp. Fireplaces from that period feature classical details such as pilasters and sport narrow mantelshelves.

## VICTORIAN

Victorians had no fear of ornamentation. The raised carved paneling, elaborate overmantels, and handcrafted glass on this master bedroom hearth will appeal to those who love Victorian style.

# CRAFTSMAN

If you love beautiful wood and handcrafted woodwork, you'll be drawn to the honesty and exposed construction that typifies the Craftsman period. Quartersawn oak was, and still is, the material of choice (fir, redwood, and mahogany are also used) for creating the simple geometric designs in the built-ins and front door of this classic Craftsman bungalow.

**COLONIAL REVIVAL**

This kitchen could be called country or rustic, but the trim details evoke the Colonial spirit. Exposed rough ceiling and support beams and simple wood window casings infuse Early American charm.

## GOTHIC

It's not necessary to carry a Gothic theme throughout an entire house. If you like the pointed arched openings that came into vogue during the Middle Ages and that are associated with churches and cathedrals of that time period, use them to make wonderful accent pieces.

## CONTEMPORARY

At first glance this contemporary interior may appear void of architectural details. But if you love the style, you know that's not true; the details are just more subtle than those in other styles. The fireplace is offset with a simple band of white, the dark metal staircase baluster adds contrast, and the elliptical ceiling that defines the entry adds a sculptural element.

**ECLECTIC**

Blending trimwork styles to suit the environment and your personality adds a playful element to a room's design. An otherwise ordinary townhouse comes alive when a detailed Georgian fireplace meets the gracious curves, columns, and simple crown molding favored by Greek Revivalists.

# ■ A History Lesson

Staunch traditionalists let a house's architecture dictate trim details, inside and outside. It's a straightforward approach: Every time period from Colonial to Greek Revival to Craftsman has a unique brand of architectural detailing. The numerous wood and synthetic profiles available at home centers and lumberyards and on the Internet make it possible to create any one of them. Here's a brief overview of major architectural styles.

### GEORGIAN (1720–1780)

**Outside:** Entrances to Georgian homes are often emphasized by an elaborate doorway or a portico, and windows are almost always trimmed in white.

Concerned with proportion and balance, builders of the time used simple mathematical ratios to determine the height of a window in relation to its depth. The style is suited to brick or stone, but contemporary versions are often clad in clapboard.

**Inside:** It's all about stout columns, bold cornices, doorways trimmed with pilasters and fireplaces featuring classical details.

### FEDERAL (1780–1830)

**Outside:** Influenced by Georgian neoclassic style, Federal residences are distinguished by their use of plainer surfaces and less pronounced detailing. Fanlights over the front door are very common, as

are the signature window shutters and a portico supported by columns flanking the front door.

**Inside:** Following the exterior shift toward simplicity, interior columns and pilasters are more slender. Ceiling medallions, botanical-inspired friezes, and horizontal bands of decoration running along the wall are common features.

## GREEK REVIVAL (1820–1860)

**Outside:** Borrowing from the formal symmetry of the classic Greek temple, Greek Revival homes feature prominent two-story porticos with massive columns often topped with decorative capitals. The windows are recessed, and chimneys are tucked out of sight.

**Inside:** The sense of order established outside continues inside with well-proportioned spaces and tall walls capped with fairly plain reeded or fluted molding. Dramatic windows that extend to the floor are typical.

## VICTORIAN (1840–1905)

**Outside:** After decades of orderly neoclassical design, the Victorian Era (named for England's renowned queen) ushered in an ideal of abundance. The rising middle class embraced all manner of architectural ornamentation. Four house styles are associated with the period: Gothic Revival, Italianate, Second Empire, and Queen Anne. Perhaps the most easily recognized, Queen Anne-style homes boast towers, turrets, and wraparound porches.

**Inside:** The Victorians used stained woods like oak and mahogany with abandon. The ornamentation so prevalent on the exteriors shows up on interiors as ceilings bordered with bold cornices and decorative carved elements on door and window casings.

## CRAFTSMAN (1890–1920)

**Outside:** Popularized at the turn of the 20th century by architects and furniture designers Gustav Stickley, William Morris, and others, the Craftsman-style bungalow is meant to be devoid of ornamentation and reduced to its simplest form. Look for a low-slung gabled roof and full or partial wide front porches framed by tapered columns.

**Inside:** Craftsman architecture introduced the idea of the open floor plan. Beautiful handcrafted woodwork in the form of wainscoting, built-in cabinetry, and columns used as room dividers, make the open spaces feel warm and cozy.

## COLONIAL REVIVAL (1880–1940)

**Outside:** Contemporary Colonial Revival homes embrace several architectural prototypes. Among the most popular and widely known: The classic Cape Cod with two or more matching dormers, and the Dutch Colonial which features a gambrel roof.

**Inside:** Keep it simple was the mantra of this design style that features minimal woodwork in the form of simple baseboards and crown molding. Door and window trims also tend to be plain.

# ■ Trimwork Profiles

A roomful of trimwork is made of many separate pieces. Here is a selection of common profiles used to create trim elements such as cornices, chair rails, and baseboards. While these elements enhance a room, it's certainly not necessary or desirable to incorporate all of them in one space. Baseboards often go "shoeless" (without the separate narrow rounded strip of molding at the lower end of a baseboard) when the room is carpeted. Also, it's perfectly acceptable to have door casing stretch to the floor without a plinth (similar to a column base) anchoring the end of the casing.

A wall can be finished with nothing but a baseboard or decorated with wainscoting, picture rails, and window casings. Each element, whether plain or highly elaborate, is often built from several pieces of millwork. These shaped strips of wood, plaster, or synthetic materials create the appearance of lines and curves on flat surfaces. The more curves and lines, the richer the profile. Take a trip to the local home center or your lumberyard, where you'll find a variety of cross sections of common moldings displayed on a sample board.

## COMMON MOLDING PROFILES

You'll find different molding profiles designed specifically for each trimwork application. The standard profiles are designed to suit a style as well as the practical requirement of making solid contact with a wall, ceiling, or floor.

The angle created where a crown molding (1) meets a surface, for example, works well on a wall or above a cabinet, but would be problematic as a door molding (2) where a flatter profile is best. Chair rails (3) can be fashioned from simple flat trim or be deep enough to display pictures or other small objects. Combined with an embossed molding (4) it can make a stronger decorative statement. Embossed moldings can also be used to add detail to a fireplace mantel. Insets (5) frame or accent wall panels and are a good way to add visual interest to long spans of blank walls, for example dining rooms and hallways.

Base molding (6) is often a composite of two or three profiles. It creates an aesthetically pleasing transition from wall to floor. Quarter round at the base covers any gaps and flat stock attached to the wall protects the wall from damage by furniture or passing feet.

Trim is generally available in 8- or 16- foot lengths and is sold by the linear foot so you can cut larger pieces down to the size you need. And, most profiles are offered in a variety of depths (measured in distance from the wall) and widths.

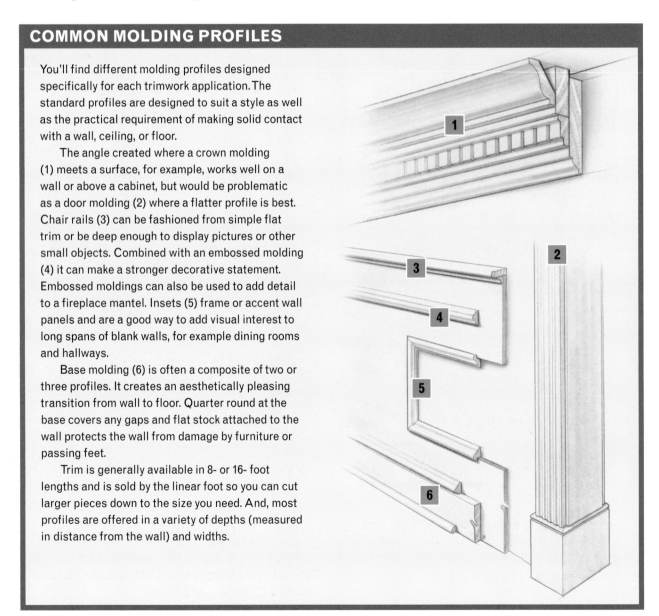

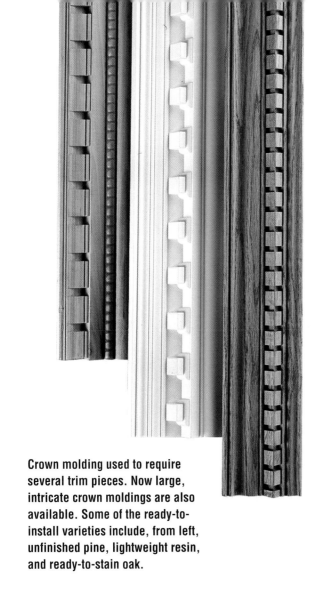

Crown molding used to require several trim pieces. Now large, intricate crown moldings are also available. Some of the ready-to-install varieties include, from left, unfinished pine, lightweight resin, and ready-to-stain oak.

Baseboards can act alone as a finishing touch for a painted wall or join forces with other pieces of trimwork to make a bolder statement. Here the flat baseboard molding is paired with a base cap selected to meld with the wall panel treatment above it and the door casing next to it. Notice how the crisp bottom edge sets off the floor treatment.

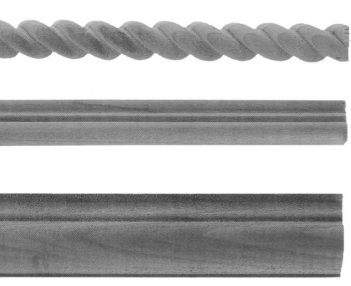

It's easy to find trim in a variety of sizes. Try 1- or 2-inch moldings like those pictured above for a chair rail. Smaller trim, such as the rope design, can be used alone or on top of larger millwork.

Typically 30 to 36 inches from the floor (one-third of the wall's height), a chair rail draws the eye around the room—an effect that can make a small room seem larger. This chair rail molding is topped with a piece of trim deep enough to double as a picture ledge.

# Adding

Just as the right necklace or belt can accentuate the lines of a simple black dress, architectural details—such as cornices, crown moldings, wainscoting, chair rails, and paneling—add richness and character to an ordinary wall. These pieces infuse a home with grace and style whether they are simple and subtle accents or elaborate focal points.

# Cornice and Crown Molding

The tradition of using cornice and crown molding began in ancient Greece. There, the exterior of temples often featured intricate handcarved molding topping elaborate friezes. These early molding examples inspired homeowners, notably in the Victorian Era, to combine various patterns in impressive built-up designs.

A less fussy approach to woodwork accompanied the arrival of the Arts and Crafts era. Later, in the International Modernist Movement, architects eschewed the use of interior trim. The postwar building boom saw the rise of ranch-style and split-level homes and the decline in the investment of trimwork. Crown moldings became less substantial, and cornices disappeared. Today's increasingly design-savvy homeowners are bringing back these architectural touches.

## CROWN VS. CORNICE

It's easy to confuse a crown molding, or *crown*, and a cornice. Crowns, as the name indicates, refer to the decorative capping to a wall, cabinet, or built-in. The crown refers to a long ornamental strip with a molded profile that is installed at an angle to its adjoining surfaces. It is often roughly S-shaped and slants toward the room's interior. Cornices are the uppermost section of molding and usually refer to the section that meets the ceiling. Cornices are often combined with crowns. Together they share the practical task of concealing and dressing up the joint where wall meets ceiling. To confuse matters, the term cornice also refers to a boxlike structure at the top of a window that hides drapery hardware.

The importance of a room has historically dictated the depth of the crowns and cornices. Parlors or reception rooms and primary bedrooms once featured ornate cornices, while kitchens and other functional spaces carried much plainer detailing. Over time crowns and cornices have become less elaborate, but many recall their Greek origins.

## INSTALLING CROWN MOLDING

If this is your first attempt at installing crown molding, start with something simple—a modest-size room with only four walls and square corners. Begin with these basic steps:

- **Take measurements.** Measure the width of each wall along the ceiling.
- **Prefinish the molding.** Paint or seal, stain, and varnish before installing. Let it dry completely.
- **Locate concealed framing.** Molding should be nailed to studs rather than to the drywall, so scan the walls and ceiling with a stud finder and make light pencil marks to indicate the studs and joists. Mark a few inches away from the wall-ceiling joint so you can still see your marks after the molding is in place.
- **Determine the installation sequence.** Work from one point around the perimeter of the room. That way you'll have only one "closer" piece to fit precisely against adjacent moldings on each end.
- **Decide on the type of corner joint you need.** When two molding pieces meet at an inside corner, irregular wall surfaces usually create a poor fit if you use mitered ends. Instead cut one piece of molding with a square end and the other with an inside 45-degree miter.

This relatively simple crown molding was painted white and allowed to dry prior to installation. It is beautifully offset by the brightly colored walls and a subtly colored ceiling paint.

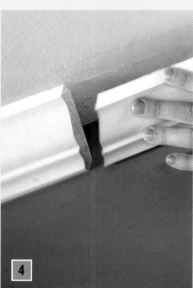

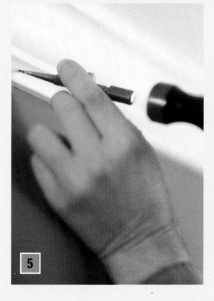

1. Use a mitersaw to cut the molding to the angle that matches the molding on the adjacent wall.

Start by precision-cutting one end of the molding and leaving the other end about ¼ inch too long. Then position the piece in place and mark the precise length to cut.

2. With a coping saw cut along a contoured edge of the mitered molding to match the profile of the molding.

3. File and sand the cut until the contour fits snugly against the adjacent molding.

Use extra blocks of molding to practice first, and make repeated test fits and trim cuts until you get it right.

Start driving nails slowly. Nail each piece in place but don't countersink the nails. If power-nailing with a pneumatic nailing gun, drive the nails in only enough to hold the molding securely. That way if needed you can remove the pieces with little or no damage. For a large crown molding, install a hidden nailer board to provide a larger surface area to nail into.

4. Splice long runs. When a wall surface forces you to create a joint between two pieces of molding, cut a scarf joint (overlapping 45-degree beveled ends) for a less conspicuous joint. The exception for this is crown molding. Making angled cuts in this stock is difficult, so pieces will likely fit better with square cuts butted against each other with a butt joint.

5. After all molding pieces are fitted properly, finish driving and countersinking the nails. Fill nail holes with wood filler or patching compound, then sand smooth.

6. Use caulk or wood filler for small gaps at corners. Touch up nail holes and corners with paint or stain.

The wall panels, window casing and crown moldings in this library are painted to mimic exotic African abura wood. Extra recesses on much of the woodwork create a richly detailed look.

Notice how the proportion of the detailed crown molding profile used above the door casing is repeated in the fireplace mantel. A similarly sized ceiling profile and detailed wainscot declare the importance of the historic Greek Revival room.

The smooth, gradual curve of this crown molding softens the transition from wall to ceiling. In a standard height room, this can create the effect of higher ceilings. White trim all around also visually expands the space, a good choice to balance the deep wall color.

### DESIGN GUIDELINES

To achieve a more formal or traditional look, think ornate and layered; contemporary styles are best achieved with fewer layers and simpler profiles. Always consider the room's size and ceiling height when choosing molding. Generally, the lower the ceiling, the more subtle the molding treatment.

A good guideline for crowns is a maximum depth of ¾-inch for every vertical foot of wall. A standard eight-foot ceiling, for example, should have a crown molding no more than 6-inches deep. Deeper molding can be overwhelming and make a ceiling appear lower. Conversely, a mere 6-inch molding would get lost on a 10-foot ceiling.

Also keep a consistent scale at floor and ceiling. Although it's tempting to install an impressive wide crown molding and economize on baseboards that are mostly hidden, the result will look better if the molding sizes are balanced.

Molding can be used even if space is tight. While busy treatments in a small space will likely make a room seem even smaller, a full suite of trim can look elegant in a tiny space when patterns are minimized or plain molding is used. For a subtler, more textural effect, paint the molding the same color as the wall or just one shade lighter.

### BUILDING YOUR OWN CROWN MOLDING

It's possible to create crown molding with as little as two pieces of trim stock. By combining stock moldings you can build a one-of-a-kind installation to suit your home's design and personal style. Start with a trip to your home center or lumberyard to look over their selections of premilled moldings.

If planning to stain trim, use the solid wood offerings available in many species. It's a good but expensive choice. If painting the molding use fingerjointed wood, wood composite, or urethane to lower costs. Urethane (as well as other synthetic materials) has the bonus of being lightweight, so it can be installed with construction adhesive.

To get a crown you like, experiment with combinations of standard molding (see "Create Your Own Crown Molding," below). If your home's architectural style and your taste mandate more substantial molding, consider the lightweight plastic options. Intricate patterns cast into molding are a great way to mimic old-world craftsmanship without the heavy lifting or expense.

All molding requires precision cutting. Be sure to have the proper tools to get the best results. Painted molding, however, makes it easier to camouflage imperfect fits. Begin with practice cuts on short pieces of sacrificial stock to perfect the cutting techniques. Corner pieces, plinths, and other transition pieces make for simpler installation than miter cuts, and joints tend to stay tight despite seasonal changes.

## CREATE YOUR OWN CROWN MOLDING

Close inspection of an elaborate piece of molding will likely reveal that it's not one piece at all, but several layers stacked to create a more complex profile. This approach makes larger moldings more affordable. Start with a base platform of dimensioned stock such as 1×4 or 1×6. This increases the profile size and provides a nailing base for the smaller pieces. To check proportions there's no substitute for applying samples to the wall to see how the various combinations look in a room. These examples give you an idea of the design possibilities.

**4-piece profile. 1.** 2" cove/crown; **2.** ¾×3½" pine; **3.** ⅝×1½" rope MDF molding; **4.** 4¾" bead-and-cove

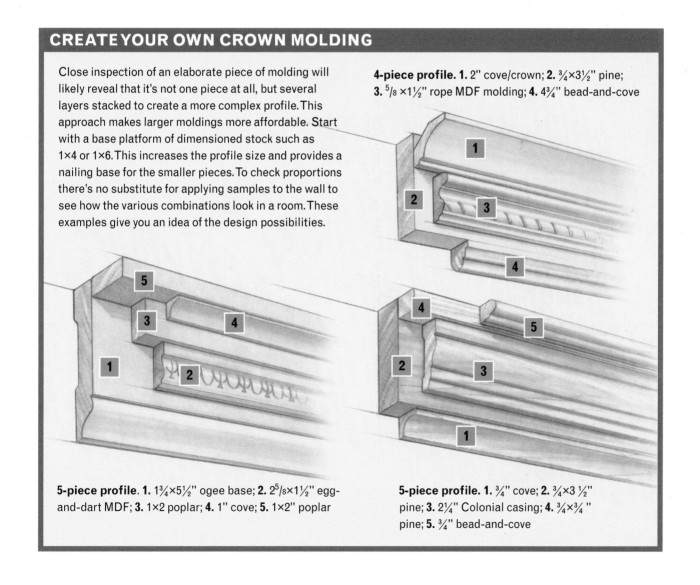

**5-piece profile. 1.** 1¾×5½" ogee base; **2.** 2⅝×1½" egg-and-dart MDF; **3.** 1×2 poplar; **4.** 1" cove; **5.** 1×2" poplar

**5-piece profile. 1.** ¾" cove; **2.** ¾×3½" pine; **3.** 2¼" Colonial casing; **4.** ¾×¾" pine; **5.** ¾" bead-and-cove

# ■ Baseboards

The significance of baseboards is underrated. More than a convenient way to cover the joint between the floor and the wall, the baseboard is a hard-working piece of molding that protects lower wall surfaces from the likes of shoes, furniture and errant vacuum cleaners. Aesthetically, it eases the transition from vertical to horizontal, adding visual appeal to the floor and the wall. As an independent architectural detail, the baseboard anchors a wall in very much the way a base provides a foundation for a column.

Georgian and Federal homes traditionally had very substantial baseboards, sometimes made of marble. Victorian and Craftsman designers also favored deep baseboards but with simpler wood profiles. Modern architecture typically features rather shallow ranch or Colonial-style molding. Whatever the style, it is essential for base moldings to complement the rest of the room's trim.

To determine if a style of base molding will work with the existing trimwork in a room, hold a sample section of the baseboard against the base edge of the door casing in the manner in which it will be installed. Make sure they dovetail nicely. Sometimes a less-than-perfect match can be fixed by installing plinths at the base of the door casings. This creates a break between the trims.

Baseboards in rooms without carpet often include a base shoe—a slender, usually rounded strip of molding installed along the baseboard's bottom edge. The base shoe is flexible and can follow floor contours to hide gaps left by the baseboard.

## INSTALLING BASEBOARD

Baseboards should be installed after the walls are painted, hard flooring is in place, door casings are attached, and any built-in cabinetry is finished. If the room is to be carpeted later, use a wider baseboard or elevate the base molding with blocks.

If the baseboard is painted a color different from the walls or will meet a finished floor, it's best to prime and paint the molding before installing it. Doing this ahead of time minimizes tiresome time spent painting while kneeling. After installing baseboard and shoe, fill the nail holes. Then apply a final coat of finish.

**This simple baseboard gets its substance from generous depth, solid thickness, and contrasting color.**

A simple white plank topped with two levels of trims creates interest and keeps this baseboard in style with the traditional window and wall molding of the room. Note the change to oak quarter-round for the base shoe to blend with the wood flooring.

## CREATING A BASEBOARD

As with crown molding it's possible to create a unique baseboard by combining stock molding.

**1.** Start with a flat or low-relief board that measures 4 to 6 inches high and install it along the bottom of the wall, tightly against the floor.

**2.** Add the cap and other accent moldings, nailing them into the main board or wall studs along the top.

**3.** Nail the base shoe to the floor so that it can expand and contract with the flooring and prevent gapping.

For outside corners use miter cuts to connect the molding; for inside corners make coped cuts.

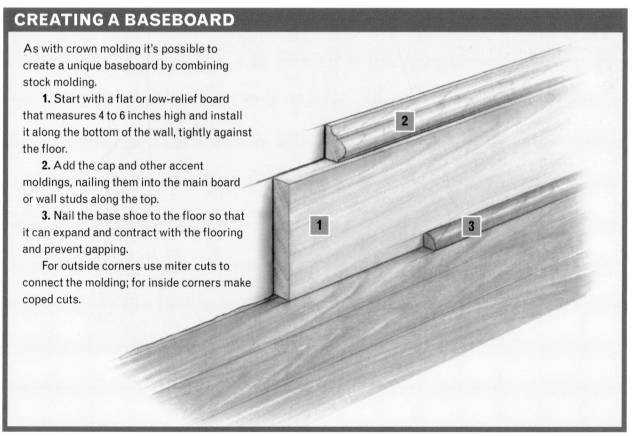

# ■ Chair Rails, Wainscoting, and Panels

As the name implies, chair rails were originally used to protect plaster walls from chair backs as people got up from the table. More at home in traditional surroundings, chair rails decoratively establish a border between two different wall treatments. This can be a wallpapered lower section and a painted upper section or two distinct paint colors, perhaps a darker hue below the rail with a lighter color above. Chair rails can also serve as a cap for a wainscoting of beaded board or wood paneling.

Rather than scarring a wall with nails or screws, picture rails feature wires hooked over molding, extended down the wall, and attached to the back of a framed photo or painting. Frieze molding is similar to picture rail: It is installed the same distance from the ceiling but is a purely decorative treatment suited to more formal, neoclassic environments. Fashioned from flat moldings with decorative relief carving, frieze molding is usually installed around the perimeter of a room.

Plate rails are another decorative feature especially popular in Arts and Crafts-style homes. Hung higher on the walls than picture rails (for safety's sake), plate rails may also have a groove running the length to hold plates in place for display.

Even if modern chair rails aren't intended to be functional, they look best installed at a height where they could prevent dings from chair backs. Depending on the chairs in the room, the rail should be placed between 32 and 36 inches from the floor. Raise or lower the height to avoid running into windowsills or other trim, as well as to suit rooms with unusually high or low ceilings. A wide baseboard provides balance.

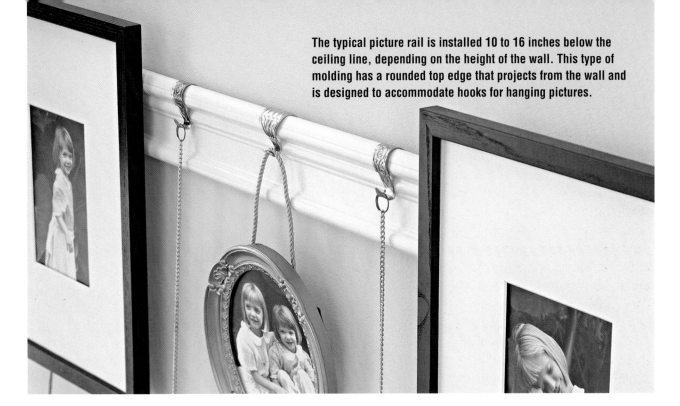

The typical picture rail is installed 10 to 16 inches below the ceiling line, depending on the height of the wall. This type of molding has a rounded top edge that projects from the wall and is designed to accommodate hooks for hanging pictures.

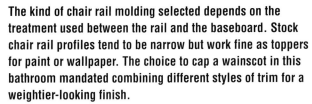

The kind of chair rail molding selected depends on the treatment used between the rail and the baseboard. Stock chair rail profiles tend to be narrow but work fine as toppers for paint or wallpaper. The choice to cap a wainscot in this bathroom mandated combining different styles of trim for a weightier-looking finish.

This Victorian-style plate rail is constructed from a narrow shelf supported by brackets. It has a groove cut into the top surface to hold the edges of plates. The matching picture rail is a nice finishing touch. The combination allows the homeowner to rotate the display without damaging the woodwork or the elaborate wallpaper.

## WAINSCOTING AND PANELS

For centuries wainscoting has appeared on the bottom half of walls to protect plaster and add a decorative touch. Believed to come from a German word, which translates into "timber that has been cut down and/or prepared," the historic wall treatment is still a popular way to add visual interest to just about any space in the house. What began as a dining room accent where there was the ever-present likelihood of chairs denting the walls has become a popular design treatment in bedrooms, bathrooms, kitchens, hallways, and stairways.

Traditional wainscoting was fashioned from tongue-and-groove wood or beaded board with a wide baseboard at the bottom. Today wainscoting is made from stone, wood, padded leather, pressed tin, or fabric. The classic wall treatment also works in various-style settings: Painted or stained wood panels enhance a country home; raised leather wainscoting elevates a library or dining room to old-world club status, and stained oak panels are seemingly essential in Arts-and-Crafts style.

The terms wainscoting and panels are often used interchangeably. To be accurate full-height wall treatments are referred to as paneling. An inexpensive way to create a paneled look is with shallow wood strips called battens adhered at even intervals to a

**Flat panels like this classic Arts and Crafts look are easy to create. Simply build a grid of wainscoting, trim out the inside of each "box" with cove molding, and finish the top and bottom with a large baseboard to create the look of expensive paneling.**

Wainscoting sometimes includes picture or wall frame designs. These divide the walls into large, visually pleasing units. Proper spacing is essential whether this feature is placed below a chair rail, above it, or both. Carefully measure each wall, making allowances for doorways, windows, and other openings. After painting or wallpapering attach the trim pieces in the desired patterns.

freshly painted or wallpapered wall. To achieve the frame-and-panel look without the intensive labor, look for prefabricated kits at home centers and home renovation companies. Shipped unassembled, the prefab wainscoting is installed piece by piece on the wall. It can also include a baseboard and chair rail.

As with trim, wainscoting and paneling are available in composites, such as MDF. Composites readily accept paint and are less susceptible to the shrinking or expanding due to weather changes that affects solid wood products.

**Chair rails are often combined with wainscoting. Similar height rules apply: 28 to 36 inches from the floor is the standard. But wainscoting can play a more dominant role in a room, such as this bedroom, reaching to picture rail height. For rooms with unusual dimensions, divide the height of the room by 3 and draw the wainscoting line at one-third or two-thirds the height of the wall.**

Always bright and refreshing, a white beaded board wainscoting with chair rail and baseboard looks good in traditional settings, especially in bathrooms. In this bath the addition of a painted shelf with support brackets provides a handy place for incidentals.

## STEP-BY-STEP: INSTALLING A BEADED BOARD WAINSCOT

A few days before painting or installing wainscoting, acclimatize the panels to your house by stacking them horizontally. Place thin blocks of wood between each sheet to allow air to circulate. This prevents excessive expansion and contraction by allowing moisture in the wainscoting to escape. Prior to beginning a project such as this, remove the room's existing base moldings. New ones will be required to complete this job. Unfinished panels should be painted or stained and allowed to dry completely before installation.

To maintain pleasing proportions in a room, wainscoting should measure one-third or two-thirds of the wall height. For example, short wainscoting is typically between 28 and 36 inches tall, including the base and cap.

The custom-milled knotty pine cabinets in this kitchen begged for window casings to match. The simple divided-light casement windows with transoms above enhance the handsome millwork.

Sometimes less is more, and that certainly holds true for the finish on these magnificent arched windows. Painting the trim and muntins the same subtle color keeps the openings from overpowering the room.

The clean-lined casings and unique muntin configuration are perfect for this modern living room and the lack of treatment allows the windows to emerge as an architectural focal point. Muntins, also called mullions, are the dividers between panes of glass. These aren't actually considered trim, but their presence or absence has a strong impact on a window's appearance; they also affect the way light flows into a room.

## WINDOW STYLES

Windows are categorized in five basic types:

1. **Double-hung windows** have two sashes that move up and down, sliding past each other on parallel tracks. Single-hung windows are configured the same way, but only the bottom sash is operable.

2. **Casement windows** swing or crank out from side hinges, much like doors. If these windows are added during a remodeling project, it's important to account for the swing to ensure that they can open freely without causing a hazard to someone walking by outside.

3. **Awning windows** are hinged at the top; they swing open at the bottom. When seated above other windows, they become transoms. This term also refers to a small fixed window above a door or another window.

4. **Hopper windows** are awning-style windows that open from the top. These are also used as transom windows.

5. **Sliders** move from side to side in a track. They're particularly useful in tight spaces—overlooking a small porch for instance—and can be styled to match casements used elsewhere in the home.

*Fixed windows* (not pictured) don't open at all. Designed without moving parts, they're less expensive to produce and serve as economical look-alikes in a gang of like windows where only partial ventilation is required.

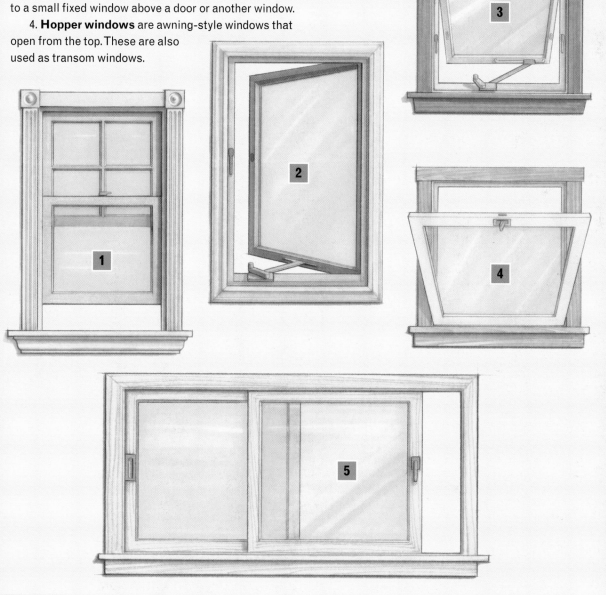

# ■ Window Shapes and Sizes

Think how boring life and houses would be if every window were a rectangle. While there's nothing wrong with classic form and the myriad of beautiful windows designed using this basic shape, variety is a goal worth achieving. Many circumstances provide a welcome opportunity to use circular, curved, and other shape openings.

**The aptly named eyebrow window adds personality to any space while capturing additional natural light.**

**A recessed, arched stained glass style window can be a charming focal point.**

**A thoughtfully placed specialty window can offer a visual surprise or draw attention to one part of a room. This round window, ideally located over the kitchen sink, does both.**

A small oval window softens the edges of the peak in a gabled wall and is a nice break from the linear shape of the windows below. It also allows light into the highest point of this bedroom, preventing the spot from becoming a shadowy recess.

# ■ Sills and Aprons

Standard windows require a trim treatment for the bottom edge. A commonly chosen option is to finish the bottom edge with a piece of flat trim that matches the side and top molding. But larger casings require something to balance the lower edge of the window, and a stool, also called a sill, is a good choice. The typical windowsill extends past the jamb (the frame that lines the window) into the room like a small shelf, and that can be an excellent place for plants or a small display of collectibles. Sills also extend onto the wall on either side of the window; this provides a place for the vertical casings to rest. Under the sill is the apron, a flat board attached to the wall and sometimes accented with decorative trim. It is usually trimmed flush with the sides of the sill.

Windowsills make wonderful display areas for plants or collectibles. If you are going to build your own windowsill consider a stock item you can cut to fit. These boards are usually $^{11}/_{16}$ inch thick. A sill fashioned from $^{5}/_{4}$-inch stock, which is usually a full 1 inch thick, will look better with larger casings.

1. *Sill.* Also called a stool, it extends into the room like a small display shelf.

2. *Apron.* The board that rests under the sill.

3. *Vertical casings.* These butt against the windowsill.

4. *Horn.* The section at each end of the sill that extends onto the wall.

# ■ Decorative Cornices

Window cornices are an easy, inexpensive way to hide unsightly curtain rods or other window treatment apparatuses. They are also a relatively simple way to add custom detailing to a room. In fact, their arrival on the American scene during the 1700s (the Georgian period) accompanied the shift from short window curtains to more elaborate draperies and a need to conceal the hanging hardware. Cornices are a wonderful finishing detail because they define or enhance the proportions of a window and make an architectural statement.

A basic cornice has three sides made of solid wood or other wood-based material and a flat top that can serve as a display space for decorative items. It's the top piece that distinguishes it from a valance, which typically has a three-sided frame with no top. Valances may also be nothing more than a fabric treatment designed to cap the window.

The standard height for a cornice is 4 to 6 inches plus the width of the casing. It shouldn't block the view, but should cover the top of the frame and part of the glass. If a cornice is too small, it will look undersized on the window. The opposite holds true—too big and it will look too heavy for the window. To get the proportions right, create a cardboard mock-up of the intended cornice and tack it to the wall for a sneak preview. This approach allows for looking at the sizing from every vantage point in the room before committing to a design.

On a very narrow window, experiment with a cornice that extends well beyond the width of the window. Add drapery panels to match the size of the cornice and watch a wimpy window grow. A decorative front panel brings character to a plain window, and window groupings may benefit from a cornice that creates a unified look.

To add visual height to a room, make a cornice taller and hang it above the window, just covering the top of the glass.

**Finishing this simple wood cornice was key to achieving a furniture look. The wood was primed and covered with a glaze and cream-color paint mixture. Then a glaze and amber-brown paint mixture was sponged on using long strokes. To create an antiqued look, the final step was applying a translucent walnut varnish with a sponge.**

For something decidedly tailored, sophisticated, and contemporary, consider upholstering a cornice. Here the nubby cotton is tufted for an ultrasleek look. Extending the cornices beyond the windows and adding drapery panels on each end makes the windows appear larger.

Less work but equally effective is a "false" cornice that meets the ceiling, eliminating the need for a finished top. It also does the job of concealing the drapery track.

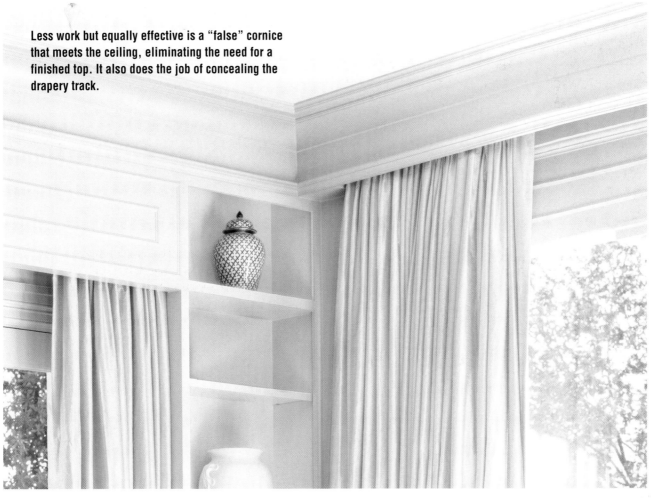

Imagine how plain the windows in this master bedroom would be without the cornices. Not only do they perform the obvious function of covering the drapery rods and hooks, the simple wood design brings the billowy curtains into focus and draws the eye upward, drawing attention to the intricate ceiling treatment.

## BUILDING AND INSTALLING A CORNICE

Basic cornices, such as this simple design are surprisingly easy to build. Essentially a wooden box, it is easy to embellish the basic design. Use trim or fabric to match the look of the room.

Measure the width and depth for the inside of the cornice box AFTER window treatments are in place.

To determine the width of the cornice, measure the drapery hardware and add 6 to 8 inches. For the depth measure from the wall, or from the window trim if the cornice will be attached to the trim, to the outside front of the drapes or blinds. Then add about 3 inches to allow the window treatments to glide easily behind the panels.

**1.** Cut the side, top, and front pieces from ¾-inch plywood or MDF. The front piece should overlap the edges of the side and top pieces with mitered joints so that no end grain shows.

**2.** Assemble the box with screws and wood glue. Then test fit it over the window, and mark the wall over the window for a 2×2 nailer or metal brackets for mounting.

**3.** Fasten the nailer or brackets to the window using header screws.

**4.** Finish the cornice by adding molding or by wrapping with padding and fabric.

When done mount the cornice by screwing through the top piece into the nailer or through L-brackets into the top piece.

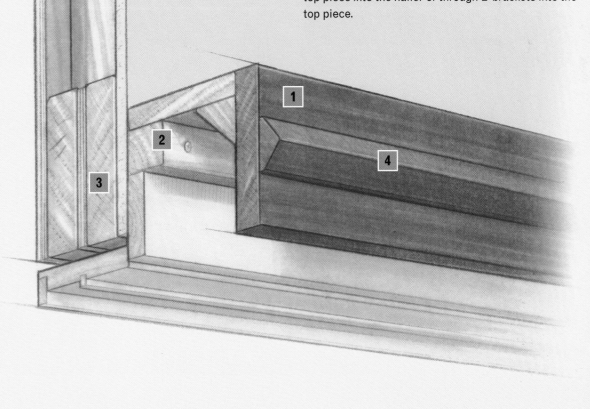

# ■ Bays and Bows

Often associated with Victorian architecture, bay and bow windows first achieved widespread popularity in the 1870s, the time San Francisco was booming. No flat window can match the sense of spaciousness that a bay or bow window brings to a room, especially a small room. These windows are unequalled in their ability to increase the reach of natural light deep into a room.

Bay windows combine three or more windows projecting outward from a room. They are usually made up of a larger center unit and two flanking units at 30-, 45-, or 90-degree angles to the wall. The more pronounced the angle, the more contemporary the look of the window. Bow windows are a variation on the bay. They have four or more window units joined at equal angles to approximate a curve.

Like their close bay relative, bow windows, distinguished by enough window panels to approximate a curve, are ideal settings for window seats. In this family room the bow window creates room for a banquette where family members can gather.

A south-facing kitchen bay window like this can serve as a miniature greenhouse. With a spacious sill, the window provides a sunny place for growing herbs or houseplants.

Changing a standard window to a bay window in this sitting room made the room feel larger, created a focal point, and also let in the sunshine. This bay features three windows of equal size set at equal angles.

In this formal dining room, a bay window opens the room to the view beyond. It also provides extra floor space to accommodate a separate sitting area.

# ■ Shutters

Shutters have been used as window coverings for centuries—first inside, then outside. Interior panels were present in American colonial times. Wealthy families would embellish shutters with decorative cutouts and other ornamentation. Today shutters are utilized more as architectural accessory than practical necessity. Many people like the clean, uncluttered appearance of shutters. These flexible window treatments provide privacy and control how much light enters a room.

Installing multiple layers of shutters with adjustable louvers over the trio of windows in this bedroom adds versatility for adjusting light and airflow. Traditional louvers are 2 inches wide or less and can be fixed or adjustable.

Most shutters are hinged with multiple panels that unfold accordion style like the ones in this kitchen or as single panels at the sides of the window. Shutters that cover only the lower half of a window are referred to as café style.

These rustic shutters add a touch of authenticity to this traditional setting. Salvage yards are fun places to hunt for old shutters to decorate a window. Or look for companies that offer new louvers with an antiqued finish.

Located at the front of the house, this dining room is shielded from a view of the street by shutters on both banks of windows. (Plantation shutters feature louvers that are at least 2 inches wide.) By covering only part of the window, abundant natural light is allowed in while ensuring privacy.

# INSTALLING SHUTTERS

Purchase standard shutters at a home center or shop for custom-made on the Internet. Before ordering determine if the shutters will be mounted inside or outside the frame. **Inside mounts** position the units within the frame with hinges attached to the jamb, resulting in a snug fit. **Outside mounts** place shutters over the window opening, with hinges attached to the casing trim surrounding the frame. Outside mounts are more forgiving if a measurement is slightly off, but they project into the room. This project features plantation shutters with an inside mount.

**1.** For an inside mount measure from the sill to the inside top of the jamb. Measure width from jamb to jamb, once about one-third of the way up from the sill and once about one-third of the way down from the top of the frame. If the window opening isn't square, trim shutters or add a shim of tapered wood under the hinges.

**2.** To get the color right, it's best to work with unfinished shutters and paint them. Before painting make sure that custom shutters fit by holding them at the window. Whether using a brush or spray painting, allow an extra day of drying before installation so that the surfaces are fully hardened.

**3.** If screws and hinges are not included with the shutters, buy them at a home center or hardware store. Prior to mounting the hardware, lay the shutters on the floor to check that they are right side up. Attach hinges about 4 inches from the top and 4 inches from the bottom. Always drill pilot holes at the spots where screws will be attached, taking care not to drill completely through the shutter frame.

**4.** Before attaching a hinged shutter to a frame, hold it in place to determine where pilot holes will be drilled for the hardware. There must be a slight gap between the shutter and the window frame at the top and bottom. Pull shutters forward enough to allow them to swing easily. Mark the spot for hinge holes and drill pilot holes. Next hold the shutter up and attach screws at the pilot holes. If a latch is desired, drill pilot holes, then attach hardware.

# Doors and

# 4

# Wall Openings

Doors provide access to and privacy for rooms. Beyond this practical function the architectural and decorative importance of doors, open arches, and passageways is significant too. To fully enjoy the value of beautifully trimmed doors and entryways, think of them as oversize picture frames that beckon you to enter a room.

# ■ Door Casings

Similar to window design (see "Window Wise," page 44), door casings have a strong impact on the style, appearance, and proportion of an opening. Door casings consist of vertical and horizontal pieces of trim, usually similar to the window casings in the same room. The horizontal piece is the head casing, and the vertical sections are the side casings.

Casings are nailed into the edge of the door frame, or jamb, and have the practical application of covering the gap between drywall and the door while helping to hold the frame in the opening.

There are a few methods for joining the head and side casings. One is to unite them with a decorative corner block, such as a rosette that combines a decorative edge treatment with the rosette center. Another is to miter side and head casings at the corner (see "Adding Style with Door Casings" on page 69).

Rectangular blocks, or plinths, sit at the bottom of the side casing where the baseboard meets the door trim. The side casing can also extend to the floor, where the baseboard butts into it for a clean line.

**The corner block came into vogue during the Victorian era, adding a decorative element to door casings. Slightly wider and thicker than the casing, corner blocks are the most forgiving way to frame the corner of a door or window.**

**Perfect in a Victorian or traditional setting, these decorative carved blocks add visual interest and break up the long lines of the archway, window, and door molding.**

Door casings are often tapered—the casing is thicker at the outer edge and thinner closer to the door opening. Recessing the trim inward focuses attention on the view beyond the door. Repeating the same molding pattern in the next opening draws you into the adjacent room.

Even in a contemporary environment where trimwork is minimal, the right casings make a difference. In this dining room, the matching head and vertical casings are painted the same color as the walls, creating a subtle frame for the modern French doors.

Older homes with low, sloping ceilings can have barely enough room for a door. When that happens it's best to fit the casing to the contours of the space for a clean appearance.

## ADDING STYLE WITH DOOR CASINGS

Decorative trimwork adds definition to door frames, and ties together different sizes and types of openings.

Many builder homes feature inexpensive plain, door trim that's mitered at the corners. It can be easily upgraded by wrapping it with a stock trim from a home center or lumberyard. Simply add an edge of trim molding on the perimeter of the casing face.

Installing a plain or decorative rosette block at the top corners where the head and side casings join results in a Victorian look.

In an Arts and Crafts setting, add a layer of thin, horizontal bead molding between the side and head casing and top the head casing with a piece of crown molding.

Turn the Arts and Crafts profile into a neoclassical one by using fluted stock trim for the side casings.

**Basic**

**Victorian**

**Neoclassical**

**Arts and Crafts**

Plain, flat trim was the right choice for a 1940s cottage-style home where the simple pattern used on the door frame matches the trim on the walls. The extra wide head casing balances the reeded-glass pocket doors.

The curved white door frame matches the elegance of the shaped window above the French doors. The casing is actually three pieces: two simple strips of side casing capped with a more complex arched header.

A pair of fluted pilasters topped with a divided-light transom frames the opening between the breakfast and living rooms. For continuity the pilasters are repeated at either end of the wall of windows. An extra-wide head casing capped with crown molding and a cornice is in the right proportion to unite this complex but winning combination of trim elements.

# ■ Arched Passageways

**Curved openings** are a wonderful way to add an upscale element to any style of house, and because arches are symmetrical they are an excellent choice for just about any size passageway. Arches come with a bonus: Even one fashioned from drywall can have a finished look without any trim at all, but including case moldings or other decorative trim adds depth and elegance.

**This archway gains impact from a coat of bright paint and a cornice and baseboards finished in white for contrast.**

This elongated archway is trimmed with traditional molding and gets support from two equally classic columns. The graceful swooped arch borders the entry and is a welcome departure from the linear passageway on the right.

## MAKING THE CURVE

Thanks to the invention of flexible drywall, creating an archway is not exceptionally difficult. The hard part is bending the trim.

One method is to laminate it using thin strips of relatively pliable wood and cutting slots of uniform depth into the backside of the wood that allow it to bend and describe the arch. It's critical that the slots are cut at evenly spaced intervals and at the right depth; improperly placed cuts can cause the wood to crack or break. Only serious do-it-yourselfers should try this technique.

The more forgiving method is using the new generation of bendable plastic moldings available through specialty suppliers and at some retail home centers.

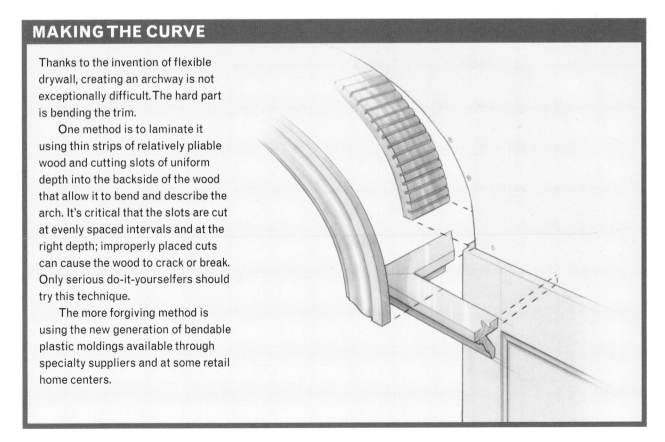

An open arch is an elegant way to transition from one room to the next. Note that arches without trim should be finished by someone with superior plastering or drywall skills because any mistakes in the plasterwork will show.

While they have the look of stucco, these Gothic arches, characterized by their pointed tops, were actually fashioned from drywall finished with rounded edges for a soft look. Arches are especially beautiful when they frame up views of other arches.

The view through this narrow trimmed arch is very inviting. It shows how important it is to consider not just the opening but what lies behind it.

## USING KEYSTONES

Arches were originally made of brick or stone built up toward the top center so that each stone or brick was supported by the preceding one.

This resulted in a wedge-shape gap at the center of the arch. The slightly larger brick or stone used to fill the space was called the keystone.

Decorative keystones became prevalent in architecture during colonial times and continue to be popular in homes of that style.

# ■ Pass-Throughs

The kitchen is the most popular place for a wall opening that allows people to pass things back and forth between two rooms. From a purely functional standpoint, a pass-through connecting the kitchen to the dining room allows the cook to hand food platters into the adjacent space without having to leave the kitchen. Pass-throughs were common in older homes for this reason, but the openings were usually small and often included a door to close the kitchen off entirely.

As lifestyles and entertaining have become more relaxed, the size of the typical pass-through has expanded considerably. While pass-throughs still offer convenience for the cook, these openings are also a way for adjoining spaces to share natural light. And, when the wall opening is generously sized, the cook can communicate with friends and family without feeling locked away in the kitchen.

Less typical but still desirable are openings between a hallway and a closed-off living room or den. Because there really is no need to pass items back and forth in these parts of the house, the cutouts function more like interior windows than pass-throughs and are a great way to add light and air flow.

Located in an older home, this small framed opening is as much display ledge as pass through. It allows the kitchen to grab light from the adjacent sun-filled breakfast room.

Before cutting a hole in a wall, think about how much visibility you want to have from both sides of the opening. This relatively high counter allows people perched on the stools to see directly into the kitchen, while visitors seated at the dining room table (behind the counter stools, not pictured) are low enough they can't glimpse any mess in the kitchen. For continuity the opening is trimmed in a manner similar to other doorways in the house.

Designing and building a pass-through is not difficult and it can be finished with standard trimwork. From this kitchen anyone can keep an eye on children in the adjacent family room via a simple opening. This one was created by wrapping the inside of the opening with jambs of finished lumber and installing casing all around in the same way a window is finished.

## MAKING A PASS-THROUGH

The construction involved in building a wall opening is easy if the wall is a partition wall and not load-bearing. A pass-through in a load-bearing wall requires a structural beam to span the opening to support the load above. This is best left to a professional builder.

This example has a horizontal sill and header attached to existing studs at both sides of the opening. Additional cripple studs increase support and provide backing for attaching the drywall. When installing the sill and header, make sure the frame is square.

After patching the drywall, wrap the inside of the opening with jambs of finished lumber and install casings as for a window surround.

To include a shelf, notch the ends of the shelf creating horns to receive the bottom end of the side casing. Next add an apron board beneath the shelf. This is similar to a sill and apron window surround.

Consider adding hinged shutters or doors to close the opening for privacy.

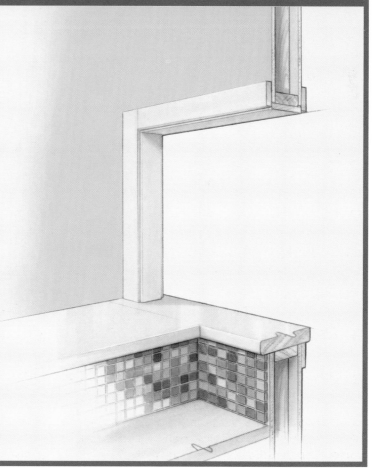

# 5

# Columns

Columns and pilasters add a classic touch to any interior. A column is an elegant way to support a beam or ceiling, frame a passageway, or create an open room divider. Like columns, pilasters add definition to walls and passageways, but because they project only slightly from a wall, they do so with a minimal effect on the space.

# ■ Column Style

The use of even numbers of columns originated with the Greeks. They insisted on an even number of columns at the front of every temple. Perhaps that's the reason that in today's home applications, columns still tend to look best in twos. And columns are visually pleasing so they're often only decorative. But columns were initially designed to hold things up, so they obviously can be used structurally. Whatever their function, column style should reflect the architecture of the surroundings.

Stout, square columns, typical of the Arts and Crafts era, flank the arched entry to this family room. The clean-line style is repeated with the over-the-seating nook and again over the fireplace.

Simple but elegant Tuscan columns provide structural support in this kitchen. Their clean look complements the plain maple cabinetry.

The capitals, or tops, of these heavily detailed columns combine the best of Ionic and Corinthian design (see "The Capital," page 83) and make a strong statement in a traditional setting.

The columns associated with the temples of ancient Greece and Rome were structural as well as beautiful and were crafted from stone. In modern architecture columns are often decorative, and because they don't require the brute strength needed to hold up a building, there are an array of material options. Contemporary columns in classical proportions are available in wood (stain- or paint- grade), plaster, metal, and cast stone.

Cast columns made from reinforced polymers, such as polyurethane and polystyrene foam, or fiberglass are budget-conscious choices.

Not all columns fit the classical mold. Prairie-style (also called Arts and Crafts, Craftsman, or Mission) pillars are stout and sometimes square with flat-panel frames stretching along each side. A bungalow-style form might be square with a flared base. A more contemporary column could be a composite of ideas, merging a fluted square panel with an unadorned capital painted in a contrasting color (see page 79).

**The Greeks and Romans considered the column to be an idealized version of the human form. The capital (1) is the head, the shaft (2) represents the body, and the base (3) refers to the feet. The decorative Doric column in this master bedroom is a typical shaft with shallow grooves. While it's possible for the various sections of a column to be crafted from different materials, shafts are typically made from paint- or stain-grade wood, while bases and capitals might be made from a composite of fiberglass and plaster. Artificial materials coupled with modern techniques make it possible to attain the look of handcarved detailing without the custom price.**

# THE CAPITAL

If design plans include columns, it is important to know what style or order you prefer. Invented by the ancient Greeks and Romans, the column is divided into three parts: the capital or top, the shaft or middle section, and the base. The capital most strongly suggests a particular order.

**1. Doric** is the oldest and simplest of the Greek styles. The capital is roll-shape and sits above a shallow fluted shaft.

**2. Ionic** design features a rounded base, a deeply fluted column, and a "feminine" capital that some believe is meant to resemble a woman's hairstyle. The scrolled form is known as a volute.

**3. Corinthian** is another feminine design. Like the Ionic pillar this order has a rounded base and fluted shaft, but the capital is highly decorative. A typical Corinthian capital features rows of acanthus leaves and pairs of volutes meeting at the top corners.

**4. Tuscan** is a variation of the Doric capital; this Roman design has a rounded base and a mound of halfround molding beneath the capital. The column shaft is smooth.

Columns need not be wall-size to make a statement. These two pairs of mini Tuscan pillars add a classical element to the traditional wood and marble fireplace design.

The original plan called for this den to be cut off from the entry by a confining partition wall. Replacing the wall with a pair of Craftsman-style pillars supported by a knee wall (also called a podium or pedestal) transformed and opened up both spaces.

## COLUMNS AS ROOM DIVIDERS

Using columns as room dividers is a stylish way to define where one room ends and another begins. And it allows the adjoining spaces to remain open to each other so light, air, and views flow freely.

One enduring room divider style is the traditional column and pedestal treatment consisting of short wing walls (pedestals) on both sides of an opening. Each wall supports a half-column that extends up to the header above the opening. For continuity the framing of the pedestal is typically wrapped with a finish that blends with the neighboring wall treatment (see page 86).

## CREATING A COLUMN AND PEDESTAL ROOM DIVIDER

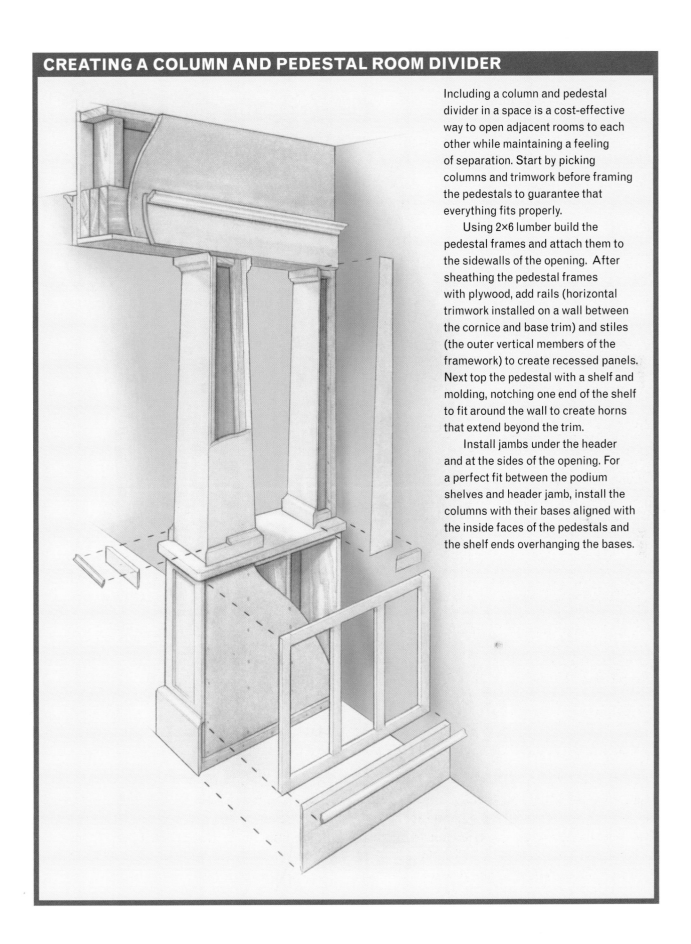

Including a column and pedestal divider in a space is a cost-effective way to open adjacent rooms to each other while maintaining a feeling of separation. Start by picking columns and trimwork before framing the pedestals to guarantee that everything fits properly.

Using 2×6 lumber build the pedestal frames and attach them to the sidewalls of the opening. After sheathing the pedestal frames with plywood, add rails (horizontal trimwork installed on a wall between the cornice and base trim) and stiles (the outer vertical members of the framework) to create recessed panels. Next top the pedestal with a shelf and molding, notching one end of the shelf to fit around the wall to create horns that extend beyond the trim.

Install jambs under the header and at the sides of the opening. For a perfect fit between the podium shelves and header jamb, install the columns with their bases aligned with the inside faces of the pedestals and the shelf ends overhanging the bases.

Half-columns on pedestals support the coved ceilings in the separate sleeping alcove and sitting area of this master bedroom. In the sleeping space the pedestals are finished with the same frame and panel treatment as the nearby wall. In both spaces the room dividers add grandeur to the overall design of the room.

A series of repeating columns delineates the foyer, dining room, and living room in this remodeled brownstone. Deep crown moldings and classically adorned columns with intricate carvings on the capitals reawaken the elegance of the old building and complement its crisp, clean-lined interior.

Instead of an enclosed, dark hallway, columns allow light to flow in while defining a passageway connecting rooms in the house. These structural supports are made of pine, lending a warmer look than white.

It's three steps up to the sitting area in this English manor-style home and the elegant space gains importance with the addition of four pillars set on brightly painted pedestals. Along with the rest of the trimwork the columns are painted a clean, crisp white to make them pop.

Combined with the curved door casing and its decorative keystone, this pair of pillars creates an open doorway that frames the view into the next room and beckons visitors.

References to classical architecture are evident in this entry hall where two sets of 12-foot-tall Corinthian pillars on pedestals provide structure for the custom frescoed ceiling.

# ▌Pilasters

**Equally important but not as familiar** as its sister, the column, the pilaster can add much to a home's interior architecture. Projecting from the wall a distance equal to about one-third of its width (a 1-foot-wide pilaster projects 4 inches from the wall), the pilaster appears to be a full-size column that has been embedded into a wall. This creates the look of a column for half the materials and less cost.

This quintessential pilaster with its perfectly spaced narrow fluting spotlights the fireplace and brings character to the entire room.

The best way to understand how trimwork features such as pilasters affect the overall look of a room is to envision the space without them. In this case the entire far wall would be far less dynamic without the classic pilasters and crown molding defining the simple window casing.

It's more common to see white pilasters, but in this solarium the pilasters are stained dark to contrast with the light upholstery and highlight the windows.

Pilasters also can be used in bookcases or fireplaces to continue the look of a room's columns.

The pilaster is essentially a group of trim elements attached to a wall or other flat surface. It follows the classical orders of the column in design and similarly features a capital, shaft, and base. Pilaster bases often include a flat block or plinth. A band of molding wraps around the bottom end of the shaft resembling a simple column base.

Most pilaster shafts are fluted boards, although some are blank or include a recessed panel. The capitals frequently include a collar or shallow band of molding. The capitals are fashioned from crown molding and other trim sporting an angled profile similar to a ceiling cornice.

**A favorite choice for enhancing a fireplace design, pilasters support the entablature and mantelshelf.**

## THE ILLUSTRATED PILASTER

Pilasters often form the vertical supports in archways or tie into ceiling cornices. They also appear with entablatures (a horizontal assembly of trim designs) most commonly in fireplace mantels and window and door casings. The typical pilaster breaks down into these parts:

**1. Capital.** Formed from crown molding and other trimwork, pilaster capitals can be simple and unadorned or have classical styling with Ionic or Corinthian detailing.

**2. Collar.** A narrow band of molding that often appears just below the capital.

**3. Shaft.** The center of the pilaster is typically fluted with closely spaced furrows all the same length.

**4. Plinth.** Deeper and wider than the shaft, the pilaster base usually includes this flat block.

**5. Base.** A plinth forms the typical base, and a band of molding wraps around the bottom end of the shaft.

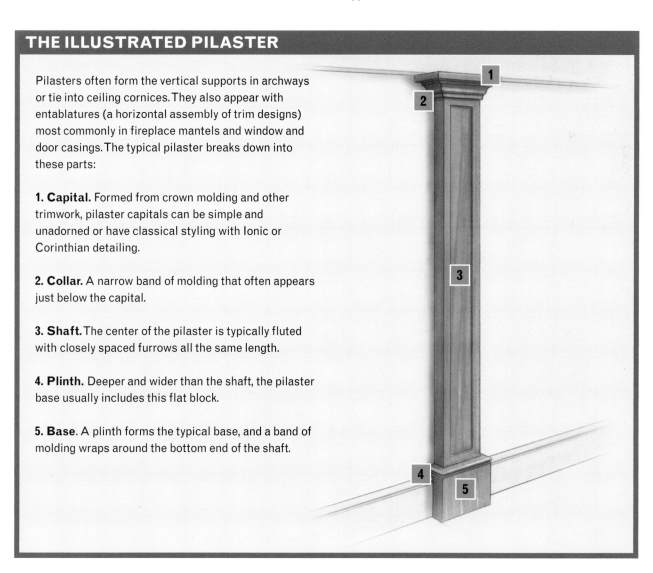

# 6

# Ceiling

The largest unused surface in any room, the ceiling is a big, blank canvas waiting to come alive. From simple exposed beams to more complicated barrel vaults to intricate plaster designs, distinctive ceiling treatment makes people look up and take notice.

# ■ Ceilings

Comprising approximately one-sixth of all interior space, ceilings can—and should—be much more than a large, flat, boring surface overhead. Ceilings provide acoustic value, help define functions in a room, and can be an integral part of the interior design. In many new homes, the main floor ceilings begin at 9 or 10 feet and can soar to twice that height in entryways and living rooms. That leaves plenty of space for beams or barrels. With a little effort, even the conventional 8-foot ceiling can be transformed with smart trim or interesting paneling. Low or high, curved or flat, most ceilings can be enhanced by selected details and/or decorative treatments.

**Because of their size beams often look best in large rooms where they can make a statement without overwhelming. The rough wood support beams on the wall and ceiling of this dining room were left in their natural state to complement the rustic decor.**

White painted beams suit this room's casual cottage style. The addition of pendants to the overhead beams draws the eye downward, giving the room a cozier scale.

## CONSTRUCTING DECORATIVE BEAMS

While some decorative beams are actually solid timbers, most are simple hollow boxes made with three finish boards enhanced with applied molding. Commonly known as box beams, the construction involves a bottom face board joined at its edges by two side boards. Make box beams out of finish- or paint-grade material.

Start by laying out the design. One way to get the proportions right is to make a scale drawing of the design along with a grid pattern for the beams. When the layout is complete, build the box frames in a workshop then install and trim them on the ceiling. Installation begins with fastening a 2× lumber cleat to each ceiling joist. Then fit the box frames over the cleats and secure with glue and finishing nails. Add molding for decoration and to hide any gaps.

Where beams run parallel with the ceiling joists, the beam layout must follow the joist spacing or add blocking between the joists to support the cleats.

Beams that run perpendicular to the joists have no such limitations.

The ends of the beams can meet walls at a wide trim board installed along the room's perimeter, or wallmount brackets can support their ends. A typical treatment for walls parallel with the beams is to add half-beams that give the appearance of being partially covered by the wall. A similar effect can be created at perpendicular walls, with a proportionately larger beam that appears to hold up the ends of the regular beams. Another possibility is to incorporate a partial-beam detail into a built-up cornice treatment.

Finish beams with the stain or paint choice that makes the most sense with the architecture and decor. A richly stained beam will have a classic look, painted beams can blend or contrast with their surroundings, and rough-hewn beams—perfect for rustic interiors—look best left in a natural state.

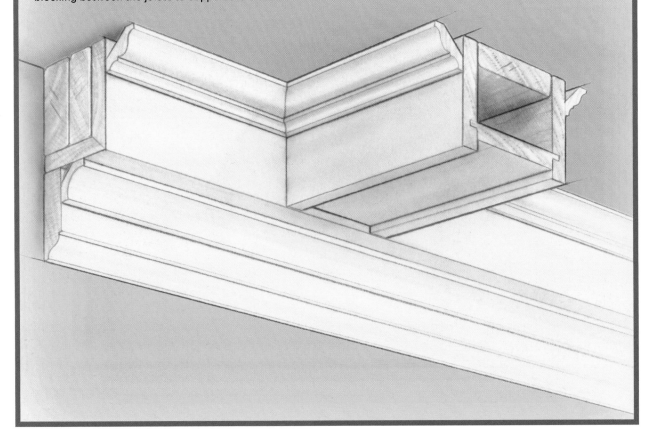

Usually found in more formal areas like living and dining rooms, a box-beam ceiling adds a touch of elegance in this room. Because box beams lower the ceiling height, they work best in spaces with a ceiling of 9 feet or higher.

## BEAMS: DECORATIVE AND STRUCTURAL

It's not unusual for an architect or builder to leave structural ceiling beams exposed. If the timbers are high grade, they lend themselves to an array of decorative finishes and add visual interest to a room. More than one remodeler has broken through a low, flat ceiling only to discover beautiful structural timbers as part of a home's roof structure.

Exposed beams can be stained to match or contrast with the ceiling, whitewashed to blend with the surroundings, painted in an array of colors, or left natural for a rustic look. Beams running lengthwise can make a room appear longer; beams laid sideways create an illusion of width. They can add to the soaring effect of a cathedral ceiling or create a feeling of protection and intimacy in a low-ceilinged room.

If the structural timbers in your home aren't worthy of exposure, don't despair. There are myriad ways to dress up a ceiling with beams. You can design a pattern for the beams that suits your taste and budget. Almost any standard plaster ceiling can get new life with a few well-placed beams to break up the large expanses of white.

Structural ceilings can show off the beauty and quality of house framing. The exposed joists in this sunroom were left natural to contrast with the wall paneling that is stained dark to match the window casings and baseboards.

# ■ Coves, Trays, and Vaults

All of these styles create a transitional element between the vertical walls and the horizontal ceiling. They also provide increased volume or height to a room. These are not simple changes, however; adding any of these ceiling types may require structural changes to a house and consulting a design professional is the first step.

**A modern interpretation of a tray ceiling with a vaulted center is created using angled drywall. Installing recessed lighting in the center emphasizes the room's height.**

### COVED CEILINGS

Coved ceilings are characterized by a concave surface that meets the wall with a graceful curve. It takes a skilled craftsperson to produce a seamless plaster ceiling. But using cove molding creates the illusion of roundness on even the flattest surface by finishing the perimeter of a ceiling with a piece of concave wood or synthetic trim and capping the bottom with simple trim molding. Most cove moldings have a gap at the back, making them a great way to conceal wiring or even recessed lighting. A cove molding's smooth, curving surface also lends itself to decoration.

A coved ceiling also refers to a lowered shelf-style soffit that edges the perimeter of the room, especially

when soft lighting tucks above it. By creating a contrast in height, the soffit makes the center area feel loftier, even though the height hasn't changed. Because this choice seldom requires structural changes, it's a relatively easy one to implement.

Simple and understated, the flawless curve of this true coved ceiling gives the formal dining room a subtle lift. The flawlessly smooth plasterwork shows how perfect this unforgiving style is in its original form.

A wide band of crown molding defines this tray ceiling and brings it into focus. Painting the interior of the tray brown to match the walls makes it an important component of interior design.

The roofline of a classic Tudor home creates many opportunities for interior spaces with vaulted or cathedral ceilings. Here a limed pine ceiling warms a master bedroom while giving it a luxuriously lofty look.

## TRAY CEILINGS

The aptly named tray ceiling looks like a tray turned upside down. Tray ceilings often have a flat center with the sides sloping in from the walls to join the level ceiling surface. Think of them as wide, overhead picture frames and you'll realize they have multiple surfaces for decoration. Trays can be trimmed with crown molding on the inverted part and around the edge that meets the rest of the ceiling; they can be wallpapered or painted with a faux finish or left plain for a minimalist look.

Tray ceilings can also create a logical place to install lighting. For soft ambience in a dining room, consider placing low-voltage halogen strip lighting in the recessed area. For task or accent lighting, find the right placement for small recessed halogen disk lights along the bottom of the tray. This tactic can also be used to highlight a work of art.

Similar to soffits, tray ceilings are simply drywall-encased frames that wrap around a room. The shallow open space is perfect for hiding the workings of recessed light fixtures.

1. Mark the tray ceiling placement by snapping chalk lines on the wall and ceiling. Be sure to mark the placement of ceiling joists and wall studs. Install 2x2 strips at the lines, attaching at joists and studs, to create a frame. Depending on the depth you've chosen, attach a 1x3 or 1x4 to the ceiling 2x2 strip to create the proper drop.

2. Attach drywall to the frame, install the recessed lighting cans, and nail metal corner bead along the edges of the drywall. Using drywall tape and joint compound, finish the drywall and allow to dry.

3. Complete the lighting fixture installation according to manufacturer's instructions, and attach decorative trimwork. Patch exposed nail heads, sand smooth, and paint.

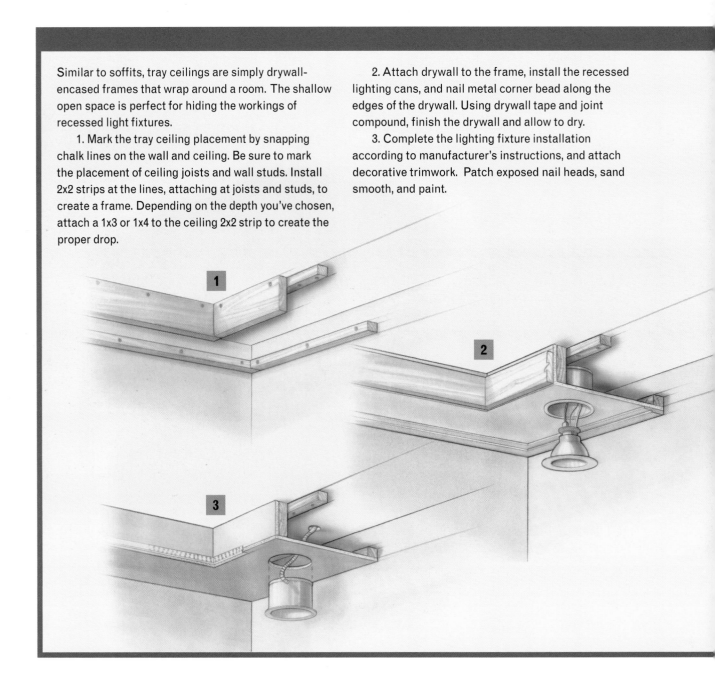

A soffit treatment is a contemporary take on the coved ceiling. Largely a cosmetic treatment, the upgrade required no change to the underlying structure, and the soffit provides a place to tuck recessed lighting. The effect is as pleasing as the traditional approach.

## VAULTS

Ceilings sloped on one side to provide height while following an outside roofline are called vaulted or angled ceilings. When both sides slant to form a central peak the result is known as a cathedral ceiling. This popular ceiling motif looks good anywhere from formal living rooms to master baths.

An arched ceiling that mimics the shape of a half barrel is known as a barrel vault. Building a curved ceiling used to involve weeks of labor because it usually had to support the weight of the structure above it. But with the invention of the drywall suspension system, the installation of these beautiful ceilings has gotten both easier and more affordable. Similar to a toy construction set, such systems allow users to handcraft preformed arcs and build the ceiling from there. Challenging for even the best do-it-yourselfers, this is a job for a contractor.

Small rooms such as this benefit greatly from the addition of a vaulted or angled ceiling because the extra headroom makes the whole space feel larger. Painting the frame ceiling enhances the established country theme.

Large rooms with soaring ceilings can feel cold and unwelcoming. This oversize great-room benefits from the addition of dark wood support beams to the steep vault.

What could have been just another bland entryway is transformed by a striking barrel-vaulted ceiling. The curved beaded board surface defines the foyer and echoes the arched transom windows above the door.

# ■ Coffers, Soffits, and Crown Molding

Americans have been adding molding to ceilings since colonial times, but coffering, the creation of gridlike compartments in a ceiling, came into vogue during the Tudor and Jacobean periods and their later revivals. The term comes from the Old French word "cofre" for box or chest.

Coffered ceilings are set with square or polygonal panels and, depending on the style of the room, can be designed to be simple and substantial or elaborate and highly detailed. The original classical coffers were fashioned from plaster and often included highly ornamented frames and panels. This style of coffer treatment can be duplicated with decorative wood beams and crossbeams laid over a flat ceiling.

A carpenter works from a detailed plan to install a coffered ceiling by combining solid or hollow hardwood beams with molding to form a grid. The ceiling itself can be left plain or may be painted or paneled.

**Intricate dentil molding cornices draw attention to the coffered ceiling in this Georgian-style home. The stunning ceiling treatment enhances the room's formality.**

Deep traditional coffers like the one in this dining room look best on a high ceiling because they lower the ceiling by several inches. In a room with a standard 8-foot ceiling, the reduction in height would make the space feel cramped.

The dark-stained timbers are further enriched by the beautiful stencil pattern on the ceiling. A similar look can be achieved with wallpaper.

Similar to beams, coffer grids need to be in keeping with the scale of the room, and consideration needs to be given to the grain, color tones, and cost of the wood selection. Poplar is a cost-effective choice for beams that will be painted, while oak, maple, and walnut are popular selections for staining.

Beams and coffers decorate the surface of a ceiling, while soffits are built-in features that add depth and interest. Many homes have some kind of soffit, often above the kitchen cabinets. The standard model is an L-shape frame built into the corner where the drywall meets the ceiling. It is generally covered with drywall and creates the perfect place to hide utility lines and structural beams and to attach the upper cabinets.

Soffits can give any ceiling a custom look. A soffit or beam that extends around the perimeter of a room creates a recess in the ceiling's center and the illusion of greater height.

**A clean-lined recessed ceiling is the perfect solution for adding headspace and defining the dining room of a modern house. Painted a deep burnt orange, the ceiling complements the organic color scheme established in the rest of the room. Track lights are mounted on the barely noticeable exposed beams.**

Trendy, contemporary spaces call for out-of-the-ordinary ceiling treatments. In this kitchen steel I-beams are used like an industrial crown molding. The result is a ceiling that looks higher than it actually is. On one side the beam caps the soffit above the cabinets.

# ■ Decorative Treatments

Flourishes of ornamental plaster graced mansions and modest homes alike in America until the 1930s. Then the time-honored craft of casting roses, acanthus leaves, French ribbons, and the occasional cherub all but disappeared. Whether it was because of the expense or because of the shift toward more minimalist architecture, most homeowners lost interest in that element.

The advent of precast plaster added a budget-conscious alternative to custom creations, and plaster treatments have made a comeback. They are a relatively easy way to add a dash of history and interest to ceilings. In rooms that boast extensive trimwork, a similar ceiling application can complement the overall interior design. Or, if a room is fairly devoid of decoration, a plaster treatment on just the ceiling can supply the finishing touch.

Plaster medallions, or the plastic or urethane look-alikes, are a great way to embellish a ceiling. The classic accents with their rich detailing and deep-relief patterns were a real favorite of the Victorians who used them to decorate the important rooms in their homes.

And medallions are easy to install. Mark the desired location on the ceiling—usually a central light fixture or ceiling fan—place some adhesive over the medallion's back, and tack it in place with a few inconspicuously placed nails or brads. Look in reproduction catalogs or online for the largest variety of styles.

**Plaster medallions are an easy and cost-effective way to add a touch of sophistication to a room. Reproduction plaster medallions are cast in lightweight synthetic materials and are available in all styles and sizes from architectural product manufacturers .**

**Like frosting on a cake, plasterwork on a ceiling is irresistible. The billowing custom ribbons adorning this traditional ceiling were squeezed from a pastry bag filled with fresh plaster and designed by a skilled artisan. Less costly precast plaster pieces are readily available from dozens of suppliers. The pieces are sold in sections and may require expert installation to hide the joints.**

A silver-leafed ceiling makes this dining room shine. It's another outstanding choice for ceiling decoration. In the evening the soft glow of the chandelier reflected in the surface makes everything in the room luminescent.

## PAINT AND WALLPAPER

If you think of the ceiling as the fifth wall in a room, you'll realize that just about any treatment used on a wall can be used on a ceiling. And, just as paint and wallpaper are simple ways to dress up a wall, they can work wonders on ceilings.

A general rule is that the ceiling should be the lightest color in the room and should complement rather than compete with the wall color. For obvious reasons—to avoid paint drips on freshly painted walls below—the ceiling should be the first surface painted. Also, it's wise to paint the ceiling prior to applying trimwork.

Wallpapering a ceiling is a terrific way to add visual interest but is not without obvious challenges. The job is best tackled by two people—one to support the weight of the paper and another to coax it into place. If covering a whole room, start with the ceiling. Matching the wallpaper pattern at the junction of a wall and ceiling can be tough, so consider choosing a less complicated but complementary wallpaper design for the ceiling.

Avoid inexpensive, thin wallcoverings that could stretch and tear easily when wet. Also keep in mind that heavier papers can be difficult to handle overhead. For the easiest installation, choose a medium-weight wallpaper.

### PAINTING A CEILING

Begin by brushing a 4-inch band where the ceiling meets the wall, then roll the brushed area. To avoid lap marks, don't do the whole ceiling at once. Instead paint about a 3-foot-square section at a time and work your way across the ceiling to the other edge. Work slowly, rolling at a relaxed pace to avoid splatters. Remember to use drop cloths.

**Paint treatments are a good choice for ceilings. The stenciled leaves on a sponged background encourage the eye upward in this kitchen.**

This lively graphic wallpaper is an attention grabber. It's a good choice for livening darker areas, such as basements, or adding interest in small spaces, such as powder rooms.

A simple wallpaper border placed about 1 foot from the wall creates a faux-tray ceiling effect.

## TIN CEILINGS

Tin ceilings were introduced in this country as an affordable alternative to the exquisite plasterwork used in European homes. Their popularity increased in the late 1800s as more Americans sought sophisticated interior design. Durable, lightweight and fireproof, tin ceilings became appealing as functionally attractive design elements that were readily accessible. Thin, rolled tinplate began to be mass produced during the Victorian era.

Similar to plasterwork the tin ceiling's popularity waned in the 1930s, but it is currently enjoying a renaissance. Today tin ceilings are used to add character and individuality to all kinds of homes. The easy-to-install panels—simply nail, screw, or staple them into place—can be painted to resemble plasterwork, clear lacquered to preserve their polished silver finish, or fashioned from different kinds of metal like copper or stainless steel to achieve a distinctly different effect.

**The busy patterns of tin ceilings left untamed by paint are best complemented with quieter tones in the rest of the room. Soft neutrals and smooth stainless-steel appliances do the job nicely in this kitchen. Note the deep trim molding wrapping the room; it creates a cove ceiling effect in tin.**

Tin ceilings are a natural choice for any style of kitchen. They work particularly well in a country or traditional setting. The clean, metallic finish of the tin complements the array of shiny and polished surfaces.

# PART II

# Making a Statement

Staircases, fireplaces, and built-ins have the ability to transform a room. A stairway can be a sculptural nexus. Fireplaces rise above the practical when they emerge as architectural centerpieces. Built-ins—from the smallest niches to welcoming window seats and whole walls of cabinetry—combine form with function.

# 7

# Staircases

The staircase is often the first thing people see when they enter a home. Whether it runs straight or turns several corners, or is crafted to resemble sculpture or elegant spirals, a beautiful staircase makes a memorable impression.

# ∎ Stairways

It's easy to take staircases for granted. Most people run up and down them many times a day without ever stopping to consider their complex construction and the number of vertical and horizontal elements that must come together to hold a staircase together. Treads and risers team up to form the steps; the handrail or balustrade gives something to hold on to; balusters in turn support the handrails and a diagonal member known as a stringer ties everything together. Many staircase designs also include a newel post, a strong vertical element located at the foot of the stair and occasionally on the landing.

A curved stair is the epitome of elegance and adds a touch of drama to any home. In this entryway the wood treads match the flooring, the risers are the same hue as the surrounding walls, and the intricate custom iron balusters supporting the handrail are a work of art. The graceful line of the stair is accentuated because it is open on one side—a design feat best left to a master builder.

As the name suggests, a straight-run staircase creates a direct path from one floor to the next without a turn. Consuming relatively little floor space, it is the least expensive style to build but needn't be devoid of character. Here the crisp white newel post and balustrade, dark wood treads, and a tapestry-look runner combine to make an elegant focal point.

A pair of matching newel posts adds to the substantial look of this traditional staircase. For design continuity the newel pattern repeats on the landing. A curved, expanded first step makes the start of the stairway even more special.

This open switchback staircase traverses back and forth connecting several floors. It features clean-lined materials to enhance the contemporary architecture. Stainless-steel cables and turnbuckles enclose the sides of the stairway, creating a more open look than if balusters had been used. Lower-level treads are wood, while the upper-level glass treads allow light to pass between floors.

The basic structure of most staircases allows for major decorative changes without rebuilding, and even the most ho-hum stairway can be transformed with a variety of upgrades and embellishments. The right trim choices can create a staircase that is simple and quiet, integrates with the architecture, or makes a grand artistic statement.

Perhaps the easiest way to improve a lackluster staircase is by painting or refinishing the existing woodwork. Slightly more challenging would be changing the entire balustrade and adding unusual balusters or a signature newel post. If your current stairs are the standard builder model of plywood topped with carpet, you can replace them with hardwood. Or take the bold move to change an entire staircase. It's possible to have a new staircase built onsite or order the entire staircase preassembled for minimal remodeling fuss.

## STAIRCASE ANATOMY

A staircase is a complex assortment of parts all working in concert to perform an everyday function while making a design statement. The staircase is also one of the most closely regulated and code-restricted elements of any house, so be sure to check codes before changing any part of the structure, including the railing.

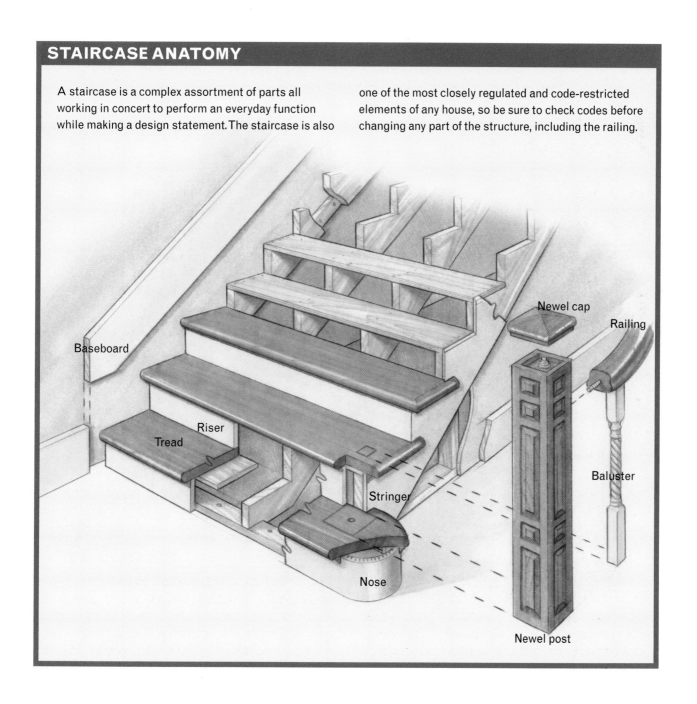

Baseboard

Riser

Tread

Stringer

Nose

Newel cap

Railing

Baluster

Newel post

# ■ Balustrades, Balusters, and Newel Posts

Almost every staircase has both a handrail and balusters—the latter referring to the vertical supports generally fashioned from hardwood that are usually turned on a lathe, a machine that shapes circular pieces of wood or stone. Balusters are also commonly formed from square or tapered spindles and slats spaced closely together, with or without decorative cutouts.

This traditional balustrade features wrought-iron balusters topped with a wood handrail. The curved, expanded first step also draws attention to the meticulously designed staircase. The newel post is further defined by additional iron balusters.

Painting this unique flat balustrade a contrasting color—such as this dark blue—makes it stand out.

While most balusters are made of hardwood such as oak, maple, cherry, or mahogany, wrought-iron supports like these can be quite elegant, contrast nicely with wood elements, and are becoming fairly common.

Classic painted and turned spindles evenly spaced support a dark-stained handrail on this gently curving balustrade. The newel post poised at the bottom is known as a box newel. The four-sided design is hollow inside and features embellishments such as painted molding, trimmed recesses, and a beveled cap stained to match the handrail.

A metal balustrade with metal cables can accentuate minimalist lines in a modern house.

This balustrade is crafted from wood to create a warmer contemporary look. The open grid goes all the way to the floor and exposes the staircase wall. A clean-lined rectangular newel post is the visual anchor.

Newel posts can take on any form such as this one fashioned in the shape of a lighthouse. Finished in a classic nautical scheme of dark stain against crisp white, this novelty newel provides a focal point for a seaside cottage.

This classic newel post design is known as a volute newel, a more formal style consisting of a central solid newel that supports a scrolling rail end and is surrounded by a column of balusters.

Balustrades refer to the entire railing—including the top handrail and the individual spindles or balusters—and are often designed to blend with the architecture of the house. Shaped handrails supported by spindles or slats characterize a traditional balustrade. Modern versions may incorporate metal or glass into the design.

Newel posts are the starting point for any well-appointed staircase and are the primary stylistic elements of the balustrade. Often the most substantial and prominent part of the overall design, newel posts are traditionally embellished. Generally around 4 feet high, a newel post can be square, cylindrical, or custom-made to some other design.

Square or box newels are perfect for adding detailing such as recesses and trim moldings. Cylindrical newel posts may display trim similar to that found on full-height columns. The crown of the newel post offers a perfect place for creative expression. It is often topped with finials in three-dimensional shapes—a ball, for example.

## BALUSTRADES: PATTERN POSSIBILITIES

The design possibilities for balustrades are wide and varied. Slats lend themselves to cutouts such as circles and squares or more decorative designs such as leaves and flowers. Cutting a shape into a balustrade requires tracing the pattern on to the slats and cutting the pattern with a jigsaw.

Three-dimensional spindles lend themselves to more complex patterns starting with grouping spindles of the same size in twos or threes. More elaborate configurations can include spindles of different sizes in repeating patterns or spindles with cross bars, crossing patterns, or insets.

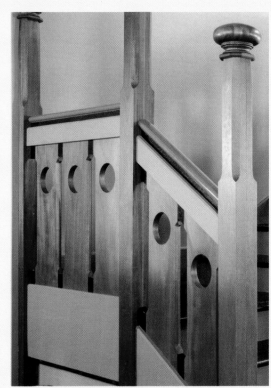

**Light flows through the circular cutouts in the balustrade slats that embellish this traditional European-style stairway.**

**Same-size spindles in alternating, repeating patterns of two spindles, then two sets of three, create the look of this traditional staircase.**

# ◼ Treads and Risers

**The horizontal part** of the stair, the surface stepped on, is the tread. Connecting each tread is the riser, the vertical component. The size and relationship of these parts to each other is critical: It determines the rise or steepness of the staircase. To prevent a stairway from being dangerously steep, these measurements are tightly controlled by building codes.

Traditional-finish stairs have hardwood treads and hardwood or paint-grade risers. The nose is the front edge of the tread, and it may be square or rounded, with a piece of cove molding below to ease the transition back to the riser.

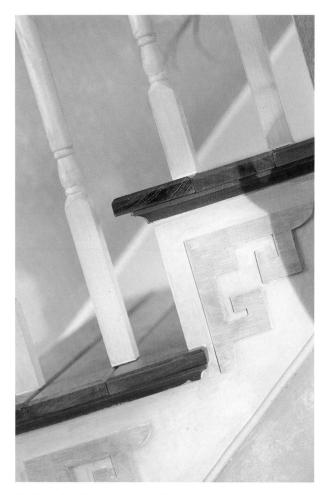

Perhaps the simplest way to dress up a staircase is with easy-to-install tread brackets. They are available in an array of motifs, or you can design and cut your own. This one is at home in a Georgian- or Colonial-style residence.

Carpet runners partially cover wood treads and risers and are good looking on any staircase. Get the same upscale look on a hybrid stair made of plywood: Leave the center of the tread plywood and cover the visible outer sections with a hardwood veneer. Secure a carpet runner over the middle of the steps.

Each riser on this spiraling staircase is fashioned from a different pattern of tile and capped with dark stained wood treads. The result is a colorful, unique stairway that makes an unforgettable design statement.

Open risers add to the crisp, contemporary look of this stairway. The design allows light to flow through which is ideal for basement staircases.

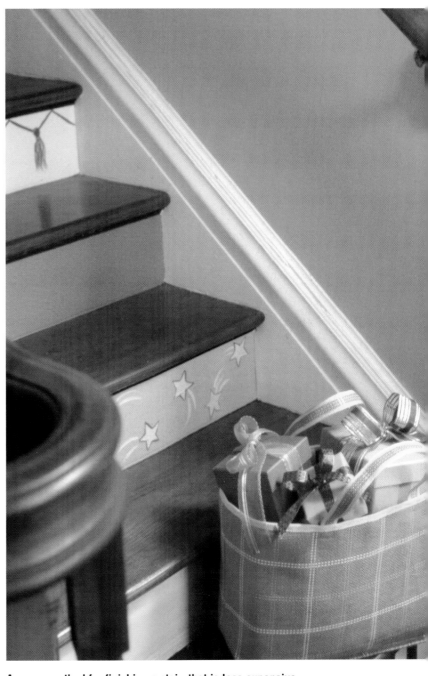

An easy method for finishing a stair, that is less expensive than tile, is to cover the risers with paint-grade plywood and paint them. Use all one color or mix different hues and patterns as was done here. The whimsical look is especially well-suited to a cottage or a bungalow.

# 8

# Fireplace

Whether refurbishing an ailing mantel or making room for a new design, a well-planned fireplace provides a centerpiece guaranteed to transform the feel of any room.

# Fireplaces

Thank the Italians for the classic decorative mantel and the basic fireplace structure used today. They developed it during the Renaissance. More than just the shelf above the fireplace, mantel actually refers to the entire area surrounding the firebox. There are four basic mantel parts: the field or inverted "U" frame that defines the mantel shape; the pilasters that flank each side of the opening; the mantelshelf that provides display space and is often supported by the pilasters; and decorative moldings. While molding provides additional personality, cove, bead, half-round, and crown molding or carved friezes also help conceal gaps, fasteners, and joints. Located just above the field, friezes can be adorned with carved wooden plaques or appliqués for even richer detail.

## FIREPLACE ANATOMY

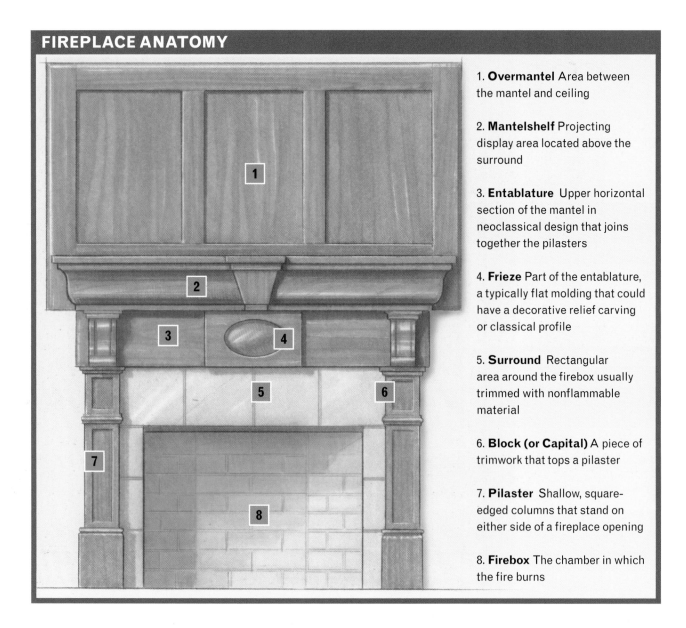

1. **Overmantel** Area between the mantel and ceiling

2. **Mantelshelf** Projecting display area located above the surround

3. **Entablature** Upper horizontal section of the mantel in neoclassical design that joins together the pilasters

4. **Frieze** Part of the entablature, a typically flat molding that could have a decorative relief carving or classical profile

5. **Surround** Rectangular area around the firebox usually trimmed with nonflammable material

6. **Block (or Capital)** A piece of trimwork that tops a pilaster

7. **Pilaster** Shallow, square-edged columns that stand on either side of a fireplace opening

8. **Firebox** The chamber in which the fire burns

This handsome cherry fireplace with a slate surround is a welcome addition to this Craftsman-style home. It features all the classic fireplace elements, including a deep mantelshelf suitable for displaying artwork and a pair of pilasters topped with decorative blocks.

137

# ■ Mantel Styles

The most successful fireplace designs enhance and complement the room's architecture. Every style has its own set of unique characteristics. Whether renovating an older home or adding period charm to a new house, research which styles were prevalent during a favorite historic period to determine whether they would work with your current home. Below is a quick rundown of fireplace characteristics from the past few centuries.

This intricate Georgian antique wood and marble fireplace surround is a salvaged piece. Instead of an overmantel, it is topped with a large painting, in the Colonial tradition.

## HISTORY LESSON

Confusing the style of one era with another is common, especially considering the overlap of time periods and the inevitable revivals. It's hard to get historians to agree on when one period ends and another one begins. To muddle things further, revivals started occurring during the 19th and 20th centuries as architects re-created styles based on historic forms, drawing from a variety of times and places. To sort out some of the key similarities and differences, here's a quick rundown of several popular mantel characteristics from the past:

**Georgian** (1720–1780): Fashionable Europeans set the trend with elaborately carved mantels paired with marble surrounds. The Georgian mantel is graceful and includes wave patterns, scrolling acanthus leaves, and iconic pilasters at the sides. Some versions feature built-in bookcases with molding to match the room decor.

**Greek Revival** (1820–1860): Sometimes called Neoclassic, the revival of Greek and Roman influence brought wide use of marble. Fireplaces may be all white with fine support columns or fashioned from richly veined marbles in black, mottled green, or gray. Those on a budget achieved a similar effect with wood painted to look like marble.

**Victorian** (1840–1905): Victorians loved ornamentation but their fireplace designs frequently took a Gothic turn and embraced medieval motifs. Built-in cabinetry, raised paneling, elaborate overmantels with spindles and fretwork—any or all of these might be gathered around the hearth to underscore its importance.

**Colonial Revival** (1880–1940): Early Americans liked fireplaces to fill an entire wall. Their hearths were often decorated with moldings and flat, fluted pilasters. In lieu of overmantels, they hung large paintings over fireplaces. Also common were wall panels framing the entire fireplace.

**Craftsman** (1890–1920): Clean, simple lines and spare geometry define the Craftsman look but not everything was rectilinear. Sinewy vines, stylized leaves and flowers, and elegant long-tailed birds in art-tile accents as well as mantels made of beaten copper and cast iron were introduced. Fireplaces often extend into bookcases handcrafted from matching wood and trim.

**American Modernism** (1950–1970): The operative word for modernism is sleek. Look for long, lean lines with few adornments. Some fireplaces in this style are without a mantel.

This living room hearth demonstrates Arts and Crafts-style artistry with the bricks stacked to call attention to the masonry.

This classically inspired fireplace incorporates a wood mantelshelf supported by corbels and topped with an arch. The combination of flat and textured tiles in the surround adds a contemporary touch.

139

Contemporary shimmery glass mosaic tiles and a stainless-steel surround make a modern mantel statement.

Sometimes a punch of color makes a mantel stand out. This traditional stone mantel stands out against a rich orange wall.

Elaborate millwork coupled with a marble surround is a hallmark of traditional European design.

Fashioned from old foundation stones and intentionally devoid of a mantelshelf and other detailing, this primitive fireplace is at home in a modern room.

# ■ Mantel Materials

One of the most enjoyable parts of designing a fireplace is choosing the materials to use in the hearth and surround: There's an absolute abundance. Wood used to be the primary mantel material for all of the elements with the obvious exception of the firebox; contemporary models feature everything from cast iron to cast concrete to ceramic and handcrafted tiles. Then there's marble, granite, slate, and a myriad of plaster and polymer options.

## HEARTH AND SURROUND

These materials are excellent fireproof choices.

*Stone and rock.* Granite, marble, soapstone, limestone and other natural stones offer low-maintenance, timeless styling. Whether cut and sanded into smooth slabs or left in their natural states, these handsome surfaces stand up to heat and bring natural beauty into your home. Because solid colors with shiny surfaces have a tendency to show

## CONSTRUCTING A MANTEL SURROUND

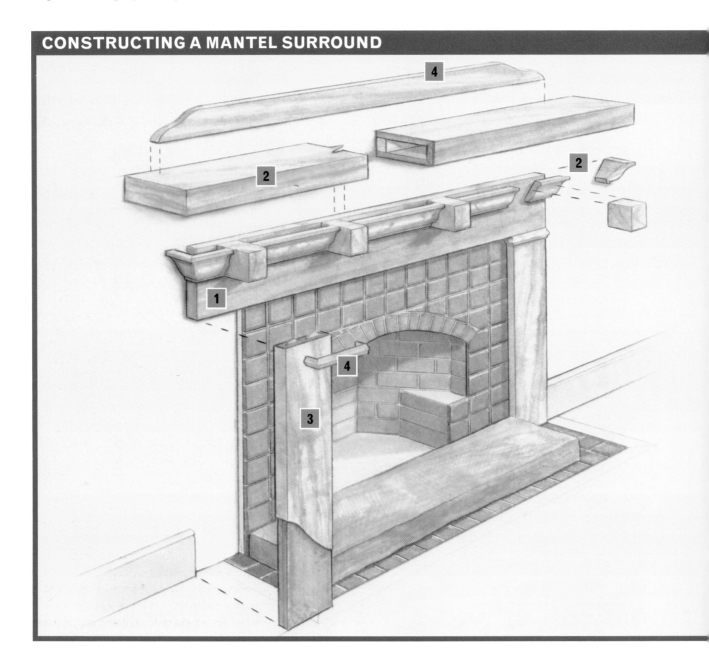

ashes and fingerprints, consider a variegated stone with a rough or honed finish to reduce upkeep.

A note of caution about using natural stone or rock for your mantelshelf or overmantel: Additional structural support will likely be needed to bear the extra weight. As an alternative consider cultured stone. It looks and feels like natural rock, but weighs only about a quarter as much as natural stone.

*Ceramic tile.* Available in an array of colors, styles, and sizes, ceramic tiles make an attractive, fireproof, and durable hearth. To disguise fingerprints and dust, select a honed finish.

*Brick.* A longtime traditional favorite, bricks can produce a range of looks depending on the type you choose and the pattern in which they are laid. Similar to stone, when planning to use brick to cover a large portion of the fireplace wall, you may need extra structural support.

*Engineered quartz.* Nonporous and fireproof, this low-maintenance material, available in tile and slab form, is made from crushed quartz and binders. Engineered quartz has a composition, weight,

Building a wood mantel is within the realm of the avid do-it-yourselfer with a well-equipped workshop. This example illustrates a four-piece mantel constructed from ³/₄-inch MDF. Two layers of MDF, laminated together with glue and screws, form the mantelshelf. This material is perfect for a painted finish. For a natural-grain look, a finish-grade plywood with a hardwood veneer will yield the desired results. Cover the exposed edges with molding.

1. Cut the side field boards and frieze board, and join them with biscuits and glue.

2. Assemble the shelf and adhere it to the top edges of the field with glue and screws. It should be perpendicular to the field.

3. To attach the pilaster and blocks, screw through the back of the field. (Molding pieces that won't come in contact with the wall or fireplace opening—such as the frieze molding—can be preassembled in the shop.)

4. Once the mantel has been mounted, install remaining molding to hide gaps.

With the assembly complete, patch exposed nailheads and paint or stain the surround, as desired.

The existing aqua tiles that form this surround were worth preserving but the original speckled gray mantel was dated. Sanding removed layers of paint from the wood and left spots of color here and there. The result was a raw, distressed finish that exudes character and was inexpensive to achieve.

appearance, and price comparable to natural stone.

*Concrete.* Concrete surrounds are nearly as durable as granite. Design bonus: Wet concrete can de dyed virtually any color and, before it is fully cured, can be stamped or embedded with decorative inlays to create any surface texture or appearance. Very porous, concrete is often sealed for protection against dirt and stains. With its rocklike color, concrete can simulate the look of a carved or a cast stone but is lighter because it's reinforced with fiberglass. Hairline cracks are common but do not affect the strength of the material.

*Metal.* Bronze, copper, iron, nickel, and steel can be sleek and modern or rustic and antique. Vintage reproductions can also be found in cast iron.

### THE MANTELSHELF

If the mantelshelf is placed well above the firebox, it doesn't have to be fireproof, allowing the most flexibility in material options. It is also the main focal point of the fireplace, so choose the material carefully and check with a design professional to see that the choice is up to code.

*Wood.* Attractive and easy to install, wood is the most common choice. New mantelshelves can be made to resemble vintage pieces with elaborate carvings and furniture detailing or left plain to complement a contemporary or rustic motif.

*Carved or cast stone.* Carved stone mantelshelves may be made of marble, limestone, granite, or slate and carved by hand or machine. Budget tip: Cast stone versions replicate the look of natural stone but at a lower cost.

*Metal.* As with metal surrounds, metal mantelshelves can be made from cast bronze, copper, nickel, iron, or steel.

*Plaster and gypsum.* Poured in molds, these delicate mantels typically feature more intricate detailing than wood and can be painted to replicate carved limestone, wood, or metal.

*Vintage.* Architectural salvage yards and antiques dealers abound with mantelshelves that create that vintage look. Larger mantels can be cut down to size, but ask a design professional if an antique treasure will pass modern building codes where you live.

**An unadorned wood mantel and a slate surround are the understated materials used for this sophisticated living room. A paneled overmantel, painted cream, complements the soft celadon-colored walls and keeps the focus low.**

This antique marble surround gained visual interest with the addition of old-world tiles, actually reproductions of pieces found in the Vatican. The handsome iron rail is architectural salvage.

Tile is a durable fireplace material with unending design options. This reworked mantel features new tilework with a running bond pattern. The decorative art tile on the chimney accents the surround.

# Mantel Makeovers

Some fireplace remodels involve relatively simple cosmetic changes. Often all an ailing brick fireplace needs is a new mantel and fresh coat of paint, while others suffer from functional problems too. If a fireplace isn't working well, consider a fireplace insert—a manufactured wood- or gas-burning unit that slips into an existing firebox. Regardless of the situation, before beginning a fireplace remodel, have the fireplace and chimney inspected for problems, such as cracks in the flue. Discuss the plans with a qualified professional who understands local building codes.

**BEFORE**

This 6-foot-wide fireplace surround features a limestone veneer, which conceals the existing brick fireplace. (The brick was discovered under the unattractive wood paneling and marble slip shown in the before photo.) The arch above the firebox and the projecting stones beneath the mantel reflect the work of a skilled mason.

This bold take on a classic design was created by an architect as part of a remodeling project to update a formerly dark and somber room.

1. The slip and hearth are limestone surrounded by a painted wood mantel.

2. Each support is punctuated with a copper plumbing cap. This inexpensive item adds a decorative element to the front of the shelf.

3. The flat panel with fins arches over the firebox and joins a pair of wedge-shape capitals.

This home's New England roots are reflected in the renovated fireplace. The existing brick surround was refaced with limestone. The commanding 7-foot-wide custom cherry mantel in a natural finish includes a set of handsome carved corbels. The adjacent firewood niche on the left is lined with copper.

Stacked stone is a durable fireplace material with tremendous versatility. By varying stone sizes and colors, an unending number of design patterns are possible. For continuity the simple wood mantelshelf and flanking built-ins are painted white.

This once grime-covered fireplace benefited from an affordable makeover involving elbow grease, a fresh coat of paint, a new stone tile hearth at floor level, and an expanded mantelshelf made from decorative moldings.

In a previous life this elegant mantel was painted blue and accompanied by an unattractive brick surround. After stripping the fireplace wood, a dark-tinted glaze was applied and wiped off, leaving a rich patina. To give the firebox opening more presence, the brick was replaced with thin slate veneer.

# 9

# Built-Ins

Beautiful and useful, built-in storage cabinets, display shelving, and window seats represent the perfect union of form and function. Including any of them in a home adds comfort and style while bringing back a sense of time-honored craftsmanship.

# and Shelving

# ■ Bookcases and Built-In Shelving

Bookcases and built-in shelving provide places to display treasures and offer practical storage solutions for organizing the overflow of items that can accumulate in a home.

Remember that style is a key consideration, and built-ins look best when they merge with a home's existing architectural details, especially its woodwork and trim.

Also take into account the fixed nature of built-ins. Unlike freestanding furniture that can be moved with ease, built-ins are a long-term commitment and should be designed accordingly. The quality of the workmanship is critical too. High-quality bookcases and cabinetry can add substance to a home, but shabby work will detract from a home's appeal.

## LOCATION

Just about any blank wall is a potential place for a built-in bookcase; however, finding the right spot involves several factors. First make sure the wall receiving the bookcase doesn't contain plumbing, wiring, or ductwork that would have to be moved. For recessed units, find a wall with space behind it. For a non-load-bearing wall, the installation will be easier because no major structural changes will have to be made to accommodate the built-in.

**Fireplaces are often prime spaces for recessed built-ins because the projection of the fireplace creates an alcove on either side. These glass-front display cabinets match the wood and style of the fireplace mantel.**

Tucked under a roof, this second-story room has a knee wall that provides the perfect spot for a recessed display case.

Set in a non-load-bearing wall, this recessed wall unit combines open shelving with an entertainment center that houses a television. If your built-in design includes electronic equipment, be sure to plan ahead. Wiring for lights or speakers will be much more difficult after the bookcases are in place.

One advantage of recessed bookcases is that they tend to make a room look larger. If extra space is at a minimum, consider borrowing square footage from an adjacent guest room or closet.

## MATERIALS

Most bookcases are fashioned from ¾-inch-thick board lumber, plywood, or MDF, with ½-inch plywood used for the back panel. For a bookcase without a back panel, be sure the unit is well secured to some kind of supporting structure—such as a wall or ceiling—or it will have very little lateral stability.

Plywood is the best all-around shelf material. A ¾-inch piece is strong enough to span about 30 inches without support. It's also economical and available in paint-grade veneers and popular hardwood veneers such as oak, maple, and walnut. The downside to plywood is its layered edge, which

**The sections of a trio of floor-to-ceiling bookcases are defined by a series of pilasters and topped with a deep molding profile. The trim was selected to tie the built-in unit to the home's Colonial architecture.**

**Handsome open or closed, built-ins in this family room repeat the grid patterns of the room's doors and transoms.**

Large bookcases like this one typically are a series of multiple bookcases installed and trimmed to appear as one unit. Like most standard units, this one rests on the floor and attaches to the wall through side and back panels.

will require an edge band of decorative molding or wood-veneer tape for a finished traditional look.

Particle board and MDF are also common, and precut shelves are widely available at home centers and lumberyards. Easy to work with, this material is suitable for painting only and requires a solid-wood nosing to increase its strength in boards more than 20 inches long.

### SIZE

To be safe, measure the items you plan to display. Standard shelves are between 8 and 12 inches deep; 11 inches is deep enough to accommodate most books. While the shelf determines the depth of the unit, length is another consideration—if a shelf is too long it may require additional supports to not bend under the load of books or other heavy items.

Doing double duty as a room divider, the floor-to-ceiling bookcases filled with collectibles line a hallway perforated by wide openings to the living room, family room, and dining room.

Although built-in implies permanence, this bookcase didn't require remodeling to accommodate it. Built of birch plywood (selected because it takes paint well) this unit is two easy-to-build modular units tied together with molding at the top and bottom and attached to the wall for safety.

This multifunctional built-in serves as a display space, entertainment unit, and home office. Adjustable shelving allows for changing display pieces and, if need be, making way for a bigger television.

Framing these display shelves in arched openings creates an elegant and sophisticated look. Measuring the Arts and Crafts pottery pieces prior to building the unit guaranteed a perfect fit.

# ■ Cabinets

As soon as the colonials settled into residences in the New World, they began building cupboards to store and display their china and pewter pieces. While some homes still include the classic corner hutch favored by our ancestors, modern cabinetry is equally utilitarian and essential to rooms like the kitchen and bathroom. Storage units have also gained popularity in great rooms, where they often act as room dividers. Regardless of where the cabinets end up, there are some basic selection questions that everyone has to face regarding cabinets: grade, price range, type of wood, and style.

**Simple flat-panel cabinets—these are dressed in blond grained-and-burled maple—not only enhance a clean-line, contemporary design, they tend to cost less. In most cases less detail on the doors lowers the price tag.**

Mixing woodtones is another way to give cabinets a unique look. In this Colonial-style kitchen, a custom black-finished hutch offsets the traditional pine cabinetry.

If you have stock cabinets, either because you are working with a production builder or you have budgetary constraints, a little creative thinking will give them a custom look. In recent years the quality of stock cabinets has vastly improved in appearance, detailing, and durability. With a small investment in trim, the most ho-hum cabinet gets a more appealing, high-end look.

### STOCK VS. CUSTOM

Stock, semicustom, and custom are the three major cabinet categories. They are distinguished by the following criteria.

**Stock:**

- Least expensive
- Lower-grade boxes
- Fewer wood choices for doors: Oak, maple, hickory, cherry, and vinyl-wrapped white doors are typical offerings
- Machine-finished: limited stain options
- Limited cabinet sizes
- Available within three weeks of placing an order
- Sold through home centers and showrooms

**Custom:**

- Most expensive
- High-grade boxes
- Greater wood choices: Exotic hardwoods such as teak and mahogany are available
- Hand-finishes: the number of stain choices increases dramatically
- Sized to fit any space
- Available in 8 to 12 weeks, minimum
- Sold through custom cabinet makers

**Semicustom** cabinets are between the other two in expense and design options. Stock cabinetmakers may offer a semicustom line with more wood and

**In the kitchen a thin strip of cherry capped with angled molding gave these stock cabinets a custom look. Cherry backsplashes complement the look. The custom bookcase in the adjacent living room repeats the style.**

finish options in a larger range of sizes. Conversely, the semicustom line from a custom cabinetmaker will have fewer features and finishes and some sizing limitations. Prices vary accordingly. To get the most out of this option, do some comparison shopping.

### CABINET STYLES AND FINISHES

The style you select for cabinets will likely be dictated by taste and house style. Most cabinet doors are completely flat, resulting in a contemporary look, or have a panel that can be raised or flat, giving the door front a more traditional look.

In stock cabinetry the least expensive wood doors (standard issue for many production builders) have a single panel of veneer plywood. A medium-priced door includes a raised panel of veneered wood over particleboard, and the most expensive stock door features a solid-wood panel.

Both semicustom and custom doors are solid wood, and nearly all cabinet lines offer wall cabinets with glass fronts, which will instantly make your cabinets appear more upscale. It's a good idea to see an entire kitchen with the cabinets you've selected. Dealers and builders should be able to refer you to a completed job or kitchen showroom. Just as it's hard to envision an entire wall of color from a paint chip, it's difficult to imagine a room full of cabinets from a sample or a photograph.

Adding fabric panels to glass-front cabinets is a simple, cost-effective way to customize them.

A built-in dresser topped with a marble slab and accented with antique glass pulls includes molding similar to architectural details found elsewhere in the bungalow-style home.

Custom cabinets cost more, but for unusual spaces or to get a specific look, custom guarantees you'll get exactly what you want. This bathroom features two floating dark-stained cabinets tied together by a low furniture-style piece designed to fit perfectly under the window.

# ■ Window Seats and Benches

A well-placed, well-planned window seat is a practical and attractive way to use the often-wasted area under a window. These inviting spaces can be uncomplicated box forms with a front panel and no storage underneath or more detailed designs featuring a flip-up seat lid, intricate doors or drawers, and specialty woods with moldings.

Key to the overall design is considering who is going to use the space and how they will use it. For example, reading and relaxing require less room (about 22 inches in depth is good) than napping, which mandates a wider berth of 36 inches. Tall window seats can appear uninviting; 15 inches is a standard height.

No window seat will beckon without the appropriate topping—the right cushions and pillows are critical to the success of the design.

Two base cabinets were eliminated to make space for this L-shape window seat. Nestled into a corner beneath a double window, the bench provides seating for family and friends to relax while meals are prepared. Because it fits flush with the surrounding cabinets, the seat adds function without subtracting square footage, and slide-out storage in the base cabinet ensures efficient use of every square inch of space.

Both the quality and intensity of sunlight throughout the day will determine how and when a window seat is used. Window treatments including shades or blinds can prevent a seat situated in direct sun from getting too warm; high-quality weatherstripping can seal a drafty window to keep out chilly air.

Thanks to paint, trim, and throw pillows, window seats can fit in well with any design style or color scheme. Bay windows are natural spots, but any window with enough room underneath is a candidate for a welcoming reading or napping spot. Window seats feel particularly cozy when surrounded by built-ins that create a homey niche.

Not all window seats require custom work. Short wall cabinets like those designed for installation over refrigerators can be a good starting point. If a window seat is slated for an existing alcove, standard 15-inch-tall and 24-inch-deep units fit well. Hide gaps at the sides using filler boards, and finish the seat by adding baseboard and other trim to conceal the windowseat base.

Inviting and space-efficient, a banquette is a type of window seat that can turn an unused corner into a breakfast nook. The typical banquette bench is 16 inches deep. When designing a banquette seat where people will be sitting for meals, allow about 2 linear feet per person.

**The benches of this family room window seat are crafted from cherry and sized generously enough to allow readers to recline or nap. Tall cabinets at either end define the space and make it feel even cozier.**

Designed to go with the early 20th-century architecture of the house, this beaded-board window bench echoes the character of the vintage bathroom. Centrally located, the window seat allows for deep drawers underneath—a convenient place to stow towels and toiletries. A cushy slipcovered top invites lounging.

An extension of a custom built-in bookcase, this bench seat is a smart way to create a finished look under the window. Loose pillows can be dropped onto the surface for seating, or stacked to leave the top open for display. Baskets of the right size are used to keep toys and tapes handy but out of sight.

## CREATING A WINDOW SEAT

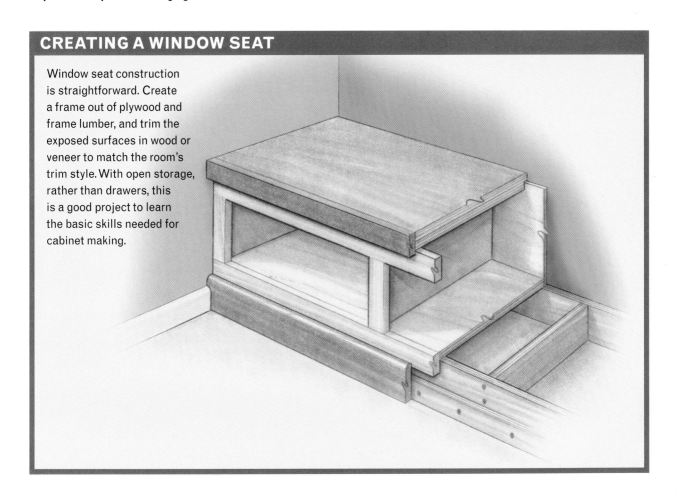

Window seat construction is straightforward. Create a frame out of plywood and frame lumber, and trim the exposed surfaces in wood or veneer to match the room's trim style. With open storage, rather than drawers, this is a good project to learn the basic skills needed for cabinet making.

# ■ Nooks and Niches

Can't tell a nook from a niche? You're not alone. Rather broad interpretations of these design features are common. Niches are defined by their gently sloping sides, while the standard nook has sides that are squared off. Utilitarian and/or decorative, both niches and nooks require cutting a hole into the drywall. Both are a do-it-yourselfer's dream.

One-piece niche models in polyurethane foam or gypsum are readily available, easy to install, and require no additional trim. Most come prefinished and can be painted, or you can buy the shell and trim separately to create your own look. Standard-depth niches fit into standard 2 x 4 walls; if you'd rather not cut, look for a surface-mounted variety. Niche and niche parts can be found through architectural

Niches are designed to put the focus on a favorite piece of art or collectible. The combination of extra molding and a painted faux finish makes this niche a fitting frame for this highly decorative sculpture.

These look like niches but with their squared sides they are nooks by definition. Strategically placed on either side of the open entryway, the pair draws attention to the table.

A good use of corner space in the kitchen, this simple untrimmed niche adds a touch of elegance to the room.

product companies, some millwork suppliers, and on the Internet.

There are no prefab nook kits because most nooks are designed to fit a particular space. A custom built-in feature, a nook can be a simple drywalled recess with no trim (easy to tackle on your own) or more complex construction requiring greater skill with materials such as stone or wood.

**Bathrooms are favorite places for niches. This convenient shower opening for shampoo and soap is edged with bullnose tile and is arched at the top.**

**A shallow, over-the-range niche keeps cooking oils and condiments within easy reach and pairs the varying textures of beaded stone molding and mosaic stone.**

A series of nooks in various sizes provides handy storage space for towels and other bathroom necessities.

# ■ Decorative Shelving

Most people like to show off special pieces of artwork, family photos, or favorite collectibles. A well-placed shelf or shelf arrangement is a relatively easy and cost-effective way to add the desired display space.

Decorative shelves can be fashioned from just about any standard construction material including wood, stone, metal, and glass. They're equally versatile when it comes to location. In addition to the obvious settings like the kitchen or a hallway, shelves can fill a space above a door or window, enhance a corner, or be placed over cabinets or in a stairwell. Decorative shelves are instant focal points that add architectural detail and a signature touch to your home.

**Shelving need not be fancy to make an impact. In this hallway family photographs are lined up on a series of long, wall mounted metal shelves.**

Architectural salvage yards are full of items that can be turned into decorative shelving like this section of an old mantel. The aged wood piece makes a perfect display for showing off plates in a dining room.

Each of these bold black shelves is slightly thicker than the one below it. The backs are hollow and fit snugly over full-length horizontal cleats that attach them to the wall.

Local home centers have everything needed to achieve this custom country look. After selecting wooden brackets and a molding for the pine shelves, attach the shelves to the brackets and the brackets to the wall. Then fit cleats between the brackets and start arranging collectibles.

Placing shelves in unexpected spots can have a big impact. These display shelves were built next to a fireplace in a space that previously had been used for wood storage.

This trio of shelves tucked in a corner of a dining room is functional and decorative.

## CREATING SHELVING

Moldings and brackets go a long way toward creating a customized shelving look. (1) Cove molding is used as a support. (2) A series of simple brackets hold up the plate rail. Note the groove in the shelf added to keep dishes in place. (3) Decorative brackets—new or salvaged—are functional and good looking.

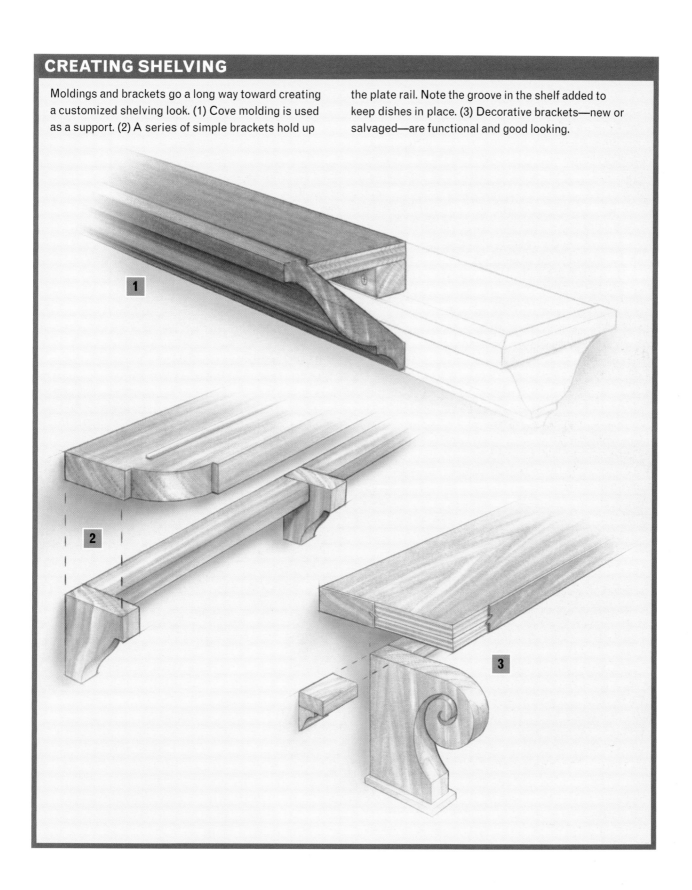

1

2

3

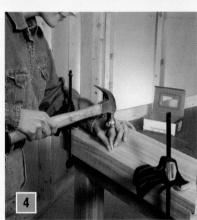

4

5

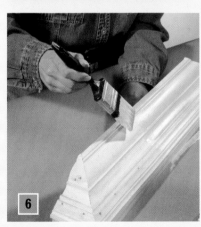

6

1. Use a miter box or a power miter saw to cut the top shelf board to length; standard lengths are 2, 3, or 4 feet. A set of three makes a nice grouping.

2. Cut the molding ends with opposing 45-degree angles. Measure and cut the end pieces to abut the front molding. Cut the sides of the end pieces that fit against the wall to seat flush against it.

3. Apply wood glue to the surface areas of the molding and the shelf. Attach the front length of the crown molding to the shelf with glue.

4. Drive finishing nails through the crown molding into the top of the shelf. Attach to the end pieces and flush to the front molding with finishing nails. Set the nails using a nail set.

5. Fill the nail holes with wood filler and allow to dry. If shrinkage occurs apply more wood filler. Sand to finish. Start with a coarse-grit sandpaper for a smooth finish.

6. Apply primer for painting, or stain and apply a clear-coat sealant. To install the shelf locate wall studs with a stud finder. Attach a cleat to the wall and fit the shelf over the cleat. Secure screws countersunk through the shelf into the cleat.

Wall shelves look good in threes and can be as deep or as shallow as you like by changing the width of the shelf board. The wider the board, the more it extends over the crown molding base.

# PART III

# Case Studies and Techniques

Choosing trimwork for an entire house is a major step. Viewing examples of homes that effectively integrate trimwork in different styles can be a helpful tool. In choosing tools, selecting the right ones for the job and knowing how to use them is a critical part of successfully completing trimwork projects of any size.

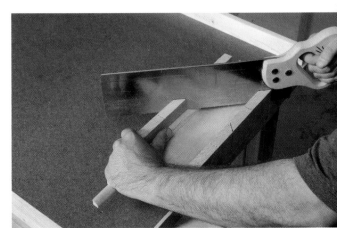

# 10

# Case Studies

Four different houses, four distinct styles—each with a different trimwork story to tell. It's one thing to learn about the power of trimwork one piece at a time—now see how they come together to make a beautiful, unifying statement throughout a home.

# ■ The Trim Difference

Throughout this book, this suggestion has been made several times: Imagine a room without trimwork. With closed eyes, perhaps you could envision the space in question without the handsome window casings or devoid of wall paneling or built-in cabinetry. To facilitate that exercise, here's what that room really looks like. Pictured below is a fairly typical builder room: lots of clean white drywall with a minimal smattering of flat, clamshell trim.

Is it a good example of contemporary design? The answer is simply "No." Good modern architecture may not employ lots of traditional trimwork, but in its place might be angled walls and ceilings or a simple fireplace mantel finished with a stone slab or

## BEFORE AND AFTER TRIMWORK

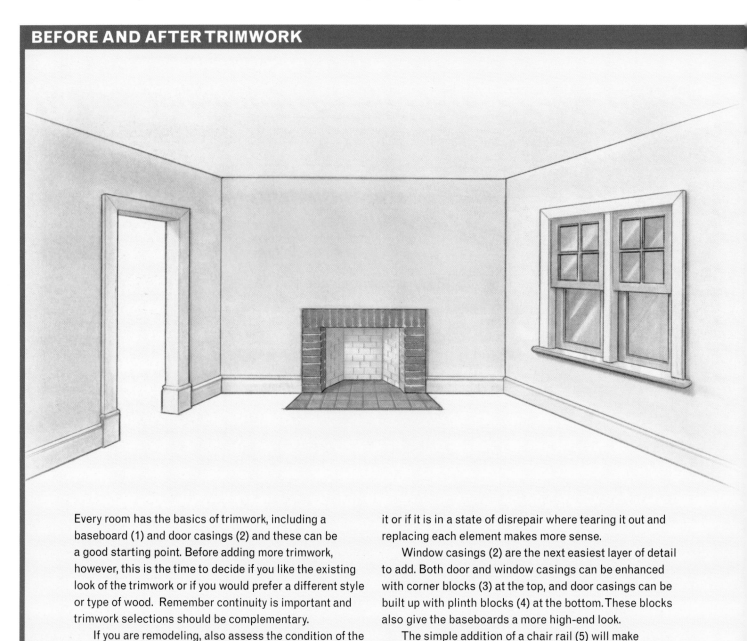

Every room has the basics of trimwork, including a baseboard (1) and door casings (2) and these can be a good starting point. Before adding more trimwork, however, this is the time to decide if you like the existing look of the trimwork or if you would prefer a different style or type of wood. Remember continuity is important and trimwork selections should be complementary.

If you are remodeling, also assess the condition of the trim and determine whether it makes sense to refinish it or if it is in a state of disrepair where tearing it out and replacing each element makes more sense.

Window casings (2) are the next easiest layer of detail to add. Both door and window casings can be enhanced with corner blocks (3) at the top, and door casings can be built up with plinth blocks (4) at the bottom. These blocks also give the baseboards a more high-end look.

The simple addition of a chair rail (5) will make those plain white walls come alive, or for more definition shimmering tiles. Or there could be open glass shelving and built-in cabinetry with flat-panel doors. Whatever the trimmings, a contemporary-design room will not be uninspired as the illustration shown on page 182.

With rooms like the one on the opposite page, people tend to find that despite their best decorating efforts, the space falls flat. Adding a warm paint color to the walls, hanging a great

lighting fixture, and selecting cozy furnishings won't solve the problem. It's no different than a well-manicured lawn—without trees and garden beds, it's just a big, flat expanse of green.

But the richness and character can be found with a few well-placed architectural details like those depicted in the "after" illustration below. The best results happen when the solution encompasses the big picture.

consider some kind of wainscot (6), and finish the wall with a crown molding (7). You could stop right here, add some wall color, and have a beautiful room that has been easy and cost-effective to achieve.

Or you could keep going and create a coffered ceiling (8) or some other kind of treatment that adds interest to the ceiling. To create a strong visual centerpiece, consider adding a fireplace mantel (9) with moldings similar to or that complement the trim added to the rest of the space.

Finally, nothing adds richness and depth to a room like built-in shelving and cabinetry (10), and they are also great space-savers. Before getting started take the time to do simple room sketches to determine what combination of trim features will have the most impact on the space and will make the most sense for how you intend to use it.

# ▌Traditional Layering

Anyone who calls an historic house home likely has affection for the window, molding, and staircase styles typically found in older homes. In this historic home, the original fanlight windows featured throughout the house remained intact and provided the inspiration for other architectural details that continue the traditional theme. To infuse a space with historic charm, consider emulating this classic trim style.

## A TRADITIONAL SUITE OF TRIM

**1.** Proportion is important. The door casings are similar in size to the window casings and ceiling cornice. Note how the French doors feature divided-light panes to coordinate with the existing windows.

**2.** A simple cornice running the perimeter of the room is a unifying feature. Painting the molding white keeps the traditional living room looking light and refreshing.

**3.** The fireplace mantel is built up with recessed molding, corner blocks, and neoclassic columns. The fluted columns are topped with Ionic capitals.

**4.** The same ceiling cornice that wraps the living room ceiling is repeated in the dining room. Using a matching wall color in both spaces is another way to create continuity.

**5.** A thin chair rail protruding slightly from the wall caps painted wood wainscot in the dining room. The chair rail serves as a border between the painted wall above and the panels below.

**6.** A baseboard eases the transition from wall to floor and, coupled with the chair rail, frames and accentuates the wainscot. The chair rail, wainscot, and baseboard work together to create a pleasing visual effect.

## ELEMENTS OF TRADITIONAL TRIMWORK

**1.** A cylindrical newel post marks the starting point of this staircase. The post is defined by a grouping of spindles to match those that form the balustrade.

**2.** In keeping with the style of the house, the balustrade is composed of traditional elements: a shaped stained wood handrail and painted lathe-turned spindles.

**3.** The wood that forms the tread is stained the same color as the floor and handrail. A carpet runner all but covers the painted risers—a good way to get a high-end look if you want to avoid the expense of all-wood steps.

**4.** The wall panel is similar to the design in the dining room but the carved rhomboid shapes are better suited to the angle of the staircase.

**5.** Crown molding accentuates the tray ceiling while helping to define the painted section of wall below.

**6.** One continuous piece of molding does triple duty as a door header, cap for the paneled wall, and window casing. Along with the ceiling cornice, the same strip of molding also defines the upper flat section of the wall. The simple effect makes the walls look taller and the whole room appear larger.

**7.** Shutters add to the clean, uncluttered look of the master bedroom while providing an attractive solution for modulating the natural light.

**8.** The same visual tricks employed in the master bedroom work in the adjoining master bath. One piece of molding serves as a window header as well as a top for the wall panel, while the crown molding draws the eye upward to the tray ceiling.

**9.** The casing is just wide enough to outline the windows while blending with the other trim features in the room. The barely protruding sill is another subtle layer of detail.

**10.** A strong baseboard finishes the lower section of the wall. The flat panel is trimmed with a simple molding profile above and a slender rounded base shoe along the bottom edge.

**11.** To keep the clean-line theme going, the tub surround is trimmed to match the wall treatment.

# ■ Craftsman Style

Beautiful handcrafted woodwork and built-in cabinetry are the hallmarks of Craftsman design. If the richness of hand-hewned wood and expert craftsmanship suits your aesthetic sensibilities but there are no bungalows for sale in your neighborhood, consider an alternate route to the style. Savvy planning can add the warmth and openness of that time-honored look to just about any setting. Note the considerable trimwork changes made in the various spaces in this house and how the relatively simple molding profiles bring the rooms into focus.

Other than lonely wainscoting and a picture rail, the original living room was devoid of trimwork and personality. While remodeling the space improved the overall layout and traffic flow, it's the new door casings, built-ins, and fireplace that really make the difference.

## CREATING CRAFTSMAN STYLE

**1.** This mantel has a custom look but was constructed from readily available materials. Off-the-shelf brackets support a mantelshelf wide enough for displaying objects. The exposed pegs mimic the Craftsman style of exposing joinery. The geometric wood panel that serves as the entablature is another cost-effective nod to the period style. A pair of flat-panel oak pilasters is stained to resemble more expensive cherry.

**2.** Clean-line cabinetry houses media equipment. The door panels are stained to match the oak floors and contrasts the darker stain—another cost-saving way to get a high-end look.

**3.** Simple flat molding defines the new passageway and interior window that reveal the sunroom. The window is trimmed with a narrow sill and has an apron below it. Both openings bring light into the adjacent living room.

## CREATING CRAFTSMAN STYLE

**1.** Reeded-glass pocket doors separate the master bedroom from an adjoining library. An extra-wide head casing gives the opening more importance.

**2.** The circular window is a welcome change from the linear elements that define this room. Trimming it in the same wood keeps the look consistent.

**3.** So simple yet so effective—a band of stained trim establishes a border between the painted wall below and soaring space above. This decorative detail prevents the sleeping quarters from feeling cold and cavernous.

**4.** The addition of a bay window creates a light-grabbing focal point while adding square footage to the library. Geometric muntins on the upper part of the window are a Craftsman-style touch.

**5.** An ample, untrimmed baseboard is another nod to the design theme that began in the adjoining master bedroom and is continued here.

**6.** The style of the warm wood moldings recurs throughout the house. In the kitchen the door casing helps frame the dining room beyond. The circular window and divided-light windows past the table emphasize the Craftsman design established throughout the house.

# ■ Classic Lines

From the crown molding on the kitchen cabinets to the bands of baseboard that run throughout, every inch of carefully selected trimwork in this house says classic. Add in welcoming banks of windows and French doors, beautifully trimmed interior passageways and carefully crafted built-ins, and the look is timeless, sophisticated, and brimming with character. Whether your taste runs to traditional or contemporary, this trimwork look works in both camps and everywhere in between.

## CREATING CLASSIC STYLE

**1.** A painted door casing frames the view from the living room to the entry and to the dining room beyond. Repeating the same framing pattern draws the eye from one room to the next.

**2.** The same simple trim pattern that surrounds the passageway encases the French doors topped with transom windows. The upper windows bring in extra light and they can be popped open to let in fresh air.

**3.** White, white, and more white. The continuing line of trimwork unifies rooms along with the consistency in the finish—and it's hard to go wrong with white. It's also possible to use a less expensive, lower grade of molding when you paint versus stain.

**4.** The portion of wall that houses the fireplace juts out into the room, and the crown molding that caps just that section of the wall adds to the visual impact.

**5.** An unexpected zigzag, a deviation from the strict horizontal and vertical trim lines established elsewhere in the room, gives the fireplace surround more impact. The same molding profile that accentuates the wall above is used to create the mantelshelf.

**6.** Two sets of divided-light French doors flank the living room, flooding the space with air and light. The same door style is used in the openings on either side of the fireplace. The combination of repeating door styles, transom windows, and clean-line molding patterns makes for a refreshing unified whole. The wood windows and doors were made to order with matching slender muntins.

## CREATING CLASSIC STYLE

**1.** More French doors, this time in the library where built-in bookshelves above and next to them add character, depth, and function.
**2.** A porthole window, similar to one in the dining room (not shown), punches through the wall to frame a view and breaks the strong linear pattern in the rest of the room.
**3.** In the kitchen, white cabinets take on a traditional air thanks to the addition of crown molding. The glass-front doors echo the window and door theme prevalent throughout the house.
**4.** Face-frame cabinets feature a frame around the front of the door and are a little more formal than their frameless cousins. Even though the kitchen is totally separate, the choice to continue the white theme results in this room looking as light and fresh as the rest of the house.
**5.** Face-frame doors and drawers similar to those in the kitchen front the spacesaving built-ins in the master bedroom.
**6.** An unusually shaped mantel adds visual interest to the slate-front gas fireplace. A small mantelshelf provides display space, and the white-painted wood is consistent with the trim in the rest of the house.

# Contemporary Theme

**BEFORE**

When space is at a premium, taking the "less is more" approach may be the logical way to transform a cramped cottage into a clean-line, contemporary space. A reconfigured floor plan helps the rooms flow better, but the "keep it simple" philosophy for trim and built-ins allows the small rooms to live large while making a modern statement.

Divided-pane French doors and a partial wall trimmed with traditional molding have no place in a contemporary setting.

## CREATING CONTEMPORARY STYLE

**1.** Crown molding painted the same color as the walls adds a subtle level of detail in keeping with the contemporary statement.

**2.** The existing French doors might have worked well in a traditional cottage setting, but the tall, single-pane model that took their place is consistent with the room's clean lines.

**3.** Setting the baseboard off with a top molding and base shoe in a lighter color helps prevent the wall from just melding with the floor.

**4.** Raising the roof created a vaulted ceiling and the addition of clerestory windows to match the pitch of the room are part of a dramatic transformation. The window unit is framed by casings to unify the three separate windows. Painting the casing the same color as the wall subdues its importance. A lack of molding on the upper portion of the walls and ceiling results in a contemporary look.

**5.** The clean-lined breakfast area benefits from the spacesaving built-in banquette. New built-in cabinets also take up less square footage.

**BEFORE**

While the existing room boasted a generous expanse of windows, they were the wrong type and the lack of trim made them just plain ugly. The low ceiling and mismatched cabinetry added to the design dilemma.

**1**

**BEFORE**

## CREATING CONTEMPORARY

**1.** A bulky staircase previously took up most of what is now a cheery sunroom. In its place floating cherry cantilevered stairs bring modernity to the room.

**2.** Raising the height of the doorway between the living room and sunroom and trimming the door in classic molding makes both rooms appear larger.

**3.** Replacing a closed kitchen cabinet with a double-sided cherry room divider that provides display space in the dining room and food storage on the kitchen side makes efficient use of the space and visually connects the rooms.

**4.** In keeping with the contemporary design, the cabinetry features simple lines but is fashioned from cherry, adding a shot of warmth.

# Tools and

# How-Tos

Whether you're installing a simple chair rail or tackling a more ambitious built in cabinetry project, every job begins with the right tools and an understanding of basic techniques.

# Your Trim Toolbox: The Essentials

### SELECTING HAND TOOLS

Consider the right hand tools an investment in life as a do-it-yourselfer. They make projects easier to complete and yield more satisfactory results. It's not necessary to purchase top-of-the line contractor-type implements, but most inexpensive tools won't perform well. Instead look for good mid-priced models.

To avoid filling a work area with tools that will be used rarely, assemble a basic tool kit and add to it when a task requires something new. If it's a tool you won't use more than a couple of times, consider renting. In the long run it will likely be more cost effective. The items shown here will cover most basic carpentry requirements:

*Tape Measure.* Buy a 25-foot one with a 1-inch wide blade; this will extend further and last longer than a ¾-inch one. If you prefer a folding ruler for smaller jobs, purchase one with a pullout extension for making precise inside-to-inside measurements.

*Framing Square.* Also called a carpenter's square, this tool is used to check corners for square and to mark rafters and stringers.

*Speed Square.* This triangular square is easy to use, allows you to quickly figure 45-degree-angle cuts, and holds its shape after getting banged around. It slips into a back pocket and is handy for quickly marking cut lines on planks and framing material.

*Combination Square.* Use this to lay out 45-and 90-degree angles. Its blade slides for adjustment.

*T-bevel.* Also called a sliding bevel gauge, measures odd angles and transfers them for duplication.

*Carpenter's Level.* A 2- or 4-foot model works well to plumb and level most projects. For a little more investment in your tool box, choose a laser level to to check existing floors and ceilings for level. It works by projecting a level beam of light that you can read and mark on any surface in sight of the tool.

*Plumb Bob.* Use this to establish true vertical lines.

*Chalk Line.* Snap long, straight lines with this tool. Also doubles as a plumb bob.

*Handsaw.* Even if you do most cutting with power tools, a handsaw comes in handy, especially a smaller one that fits into a toolbox.

*Miter Box and Backsaw.* A backsaw creates finer, more accurate cuts and is typically used with a miter box to cut precise angles.

*Coping Saw.* A good tool for cutting intricate and precise curves in thin materials.

*Wood Chisel.* Choose chisels with metal, shaped handles for cutting mortises and making rough notches in places where saws will not reach.

*Utility Knife.* Keep one of these close at hand for razor-sharp cuts. Most people prefer one with a retractable blade.

*Block Plane.* Use this tool for shaving the ends and angles on larger pieces of wood.

*Nail Hammer.* The most popular model weighs 16 ounces and has curved claws. Pick a model that is comfortable and solidly built.

*Awl and Nail Set.* Use the awl to mark the spot for driving in a nail; use the nail set to sink the heads of finishing nails just below the surface of the wood.

*Screwdrivers.* Have plenty of these on hand in various sizes of both phillips-tip and straight-tipped types or buy a combination screwdriver that has four tips in one tool.

*Adjustable Wrench.* Use this to fasten nuts, bolts, and lag screws.

*C-clamps.* Keep various sizes handy for holding pieces of wood firmly.

*Locking Pliers.* These help hold fasteners or pieces of wood tight while you work.

*Tongue-and-Groove Pliers.* One of the most useful tools you can buy, so pay extra for a high-quality pair. They grab almost anything firmly and work well for pulling nails.

*Flat Pry Bar.* This indispensable tool is used to pry off fastened lumber pieces with minimal damage to the wood. It is also handy for levering heavy objects into place—like reattaching a door on its hinges.

To accurately locate wooden studs inside walls, add a stud finder to your tool box. It measures changes in the wall's intensity. Note that this tool may not work effectively with metal studs.

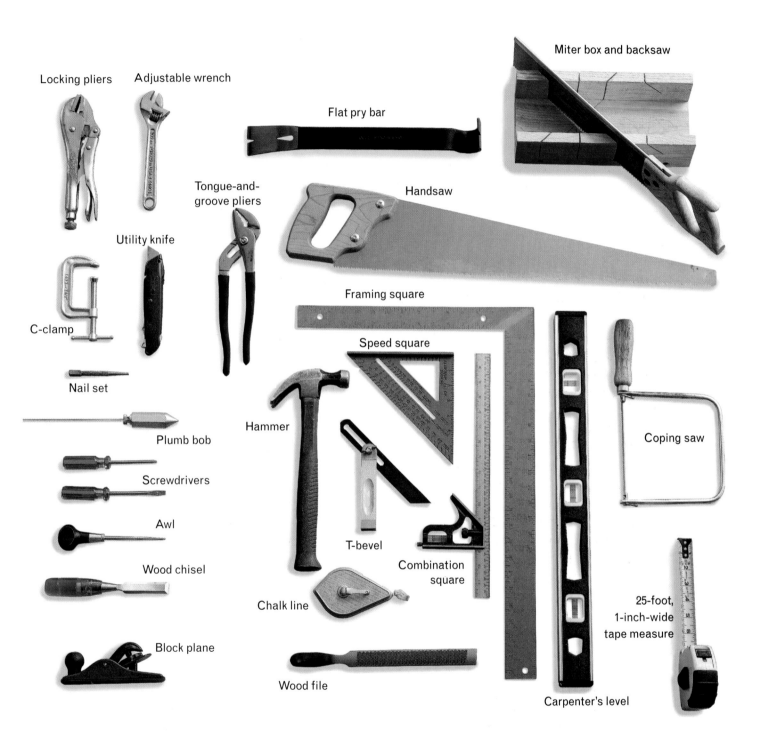

Locking pliers

Adjustable wrench

Flat pry bar

Miter box and backsaw

Tongue-and-
groove pliers

Handsaw

Utility knife

C-clamp

Framing square

Nail set

Speed square

Plumb bob

Hammer

Coping saw

Screwdrivers

Awl

T-bevel

Combination
square

25-foot,
1-inch-wide
tape measure

Wood chisel

Chalk line

Block plane

Wood file

Carpenter's level

Circular saw

Cordless drill

Random-orbit sander

Jig saw

Power drill

## POWER TOOLS

No basic tool kit is complete without a *circular saw*, a *power drill*, and a *jigsaw*. With these three tools you can handle almost any household carpentry task. Between them, the two saws can make straight and curved cuts quickly in almost any material, while the drill allows you to drive screws quickly and easily.

A circular saw crosscuts, anglecuts, rips (cuts lengthwise), and even bevels lumber easily and cleanly. Most of today's saws have a plastic housing that is surprisingly durable. Chose a model with a thick base made of extruded or cast metal. A baseplate made of thin, stamped metal can warp. A saw that takes 7 ¼ inch blades is the usual choice. Horsepower is less important than amperage and the type of bearings. A good midpriced saw will be rated at 12 or 13 amps and may have ball bearings.

A *cordless drill* frees you to work without the mess of electrical cords. Buy one rated at least 9.6 volts.

Get an extra battery pack so you won't have to wait for a battery to charge.

When purchasing a jigsaw, examine the baseplate and the adjusting mechanism. On less expensive saws, these are flimsy and eventually wobble, making it difficult to keep the blade aligned vertically. Variable speed is a useful option. A saw that draws 3 amps or more can handle most cutting requirements.

Get a variable-speed reversible power drill. A ⅜-inch chuck is suitable for home use. Look for a drill that pulls at least 3.5 amps. A keyless chuck simplifies changing bits, but some people prefer a keyed chuck for a tighter grip on the bit.

Also consider buying a small, *random-orbit sander*. This handy power tool makes quick work of basic sanding and reduces the amount of fatigue, especially when sanding large areas.

One moment's lapse of concentration can lead to serious injury when working with hand or power tools. Completing projects safely is the result of following guidelines and exercising common sense. To minimize risks, keep the following guidelines in mind:

**Use Tools For Their Intended Use Only**. Read the instruction manual to find out what a tool will do and will not do.

**Check a Tool's Condition Before Using**. A dull cutting edge or a loose-fitting hammerhead, for example, spell trouble. Always inspect the cord of a power tool to make sure it's not damaged.

**Don't Work With Tools If You're Tired or In a Hurry.**

**Alcohol and Tools Don't Mix—Ever.**

**Wear Goggles.** Wear protective eye covers if the operation you are performing could result in eye damage.

**Don't Tamper With or Remove Power Tool Safety Mechanisms**. They are there for your protection.

## PROTECT YOURSELF

Safety equipment is a must for any project. Always wear safety goggles. Even if you wear glasses, safety glasses are important because they provide greater coverage than standard lenses. Wear a dust mask or a respirator when cutting, sanding, and taking on demolition work.

Many carpentry tools are extremely loud, so use earplugs or hearing protectors when operating them.

Wear a cap to keep dust and debris out of your hair, and put on a hard hat for demolition work.

**Don't Wear Loosely Fitting Clothes or Dangling Jewelry When Working With Tools.**

**Keep Other People, Especially Children, At a Safe Distance**. Before allowing children to use a tool, instruct them on how to operate it and always supervise them as they work.

**Always Unplug a Power Tool Before Servicing**. Allow all moving parts to stop before making any adjustments.

# ■ Marking and Measuring

Getting an accurate measurement is essential to any trimwork project and the carpenter's adage: "Measure twice, cut once," is a good one to remember. To ensure the best results use the same measuring device for all measurements (a yardstick and tape measure could yield slightly different results) and take the time to read correctly. Being able to distinguish between a ¼-inch mark and an ⅛-inch mark is essential. Finally, because it's often the marking, not the reading where problems occur, be sure to make a clear mark using a sharp No. 2 pencil, the thin edge of a sharpened carpenter's pencil, a knife, or a scratch awl.

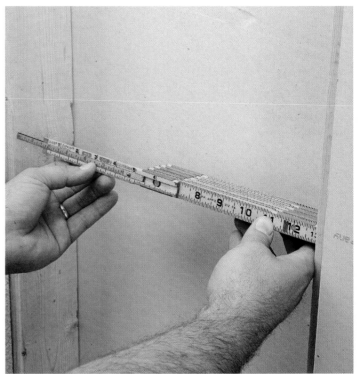

A steel tape is the most popular measuring device because it's so easy to use. The hook at the end of the tape slides back and forth slightly to compensate for its own thickness. Also note that for the first few inches of most tapes; each inch is divided into ¹⁄₃₂-inch increments to facilitate extra-fine measurements.

A folding ruler with a slide-out metal scale works best to make an accurate inside measurement. Extend it, measure, and hold the slide with your thumb until the measurement is recorded. It is possible to use a tape measure, but accuracy is difficult because it's necessary to add an amount to compensate for the length of the tape.

## NO-MISTAKE MEASURING

Even the most skilled carpenters make measuring bloopers so don't be surprised when it happens to you. Here are some common mistakes and ways to avoid them:

**Sawing on the wrong side of the line.** Cutting on the good rather than the scrap side of the line will result in a board that's about ⅛ inch short. To get it right, always draw an X on the scrap side.

**Misreading numbers.** Mixing up a 6 and a 9 can be a disaster; make sure you don't read numbers upside-down.

**Forgetting a measurement.** Get in the habit of writing down all measurements immediately and you'll never have this problem.

**1.** Marking a piece of wood with a simple line can cause accuracy problems. By the time you have your saw in hand you might not remember which end of the line marks the spot or where exactly to cut on a thick line made with a blunt pencil. For greater precision, mark your measurements with a V so you know exactly where to strike the cut line.

**2.** Your cutting goal should be pinpoint accuracy and to guarantee that, place the point of your pencil on the V, slide the square to it, and then make your line. If you need to extend cut lines across several boards, use a framing square. For longer lines, it's best to use a drywall square.

**3.** Marking a cutoff line along the length of a board or a piece of plywood requires a different technique. If the line needs to run parallel to the edge of the board and pinpoint accuracy isn't critical, you can use your tape measure as a scribing tool. Hold the tape so that a pencil laid against its ends will make the correct line. Hold the tape and pencil firmly, and pull evenly toward you, allowing the tape body or your thumbnail to slide along the board edge.

**4.** When working with sheet goods, mark the cutoff lines at both ends first. Next, snap a chalk line between the two marks, or clamp a straightedge in place and draw your mark.

**5.** Anytime you cut wood, a saw blade reduces some of it to sawdust so when measuring, it's important to allow for the wood removed by the blade, known as kerf. Generally a kerf is about ⅛ inch wide. When making just one cut, account

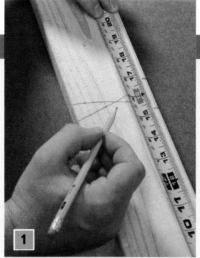

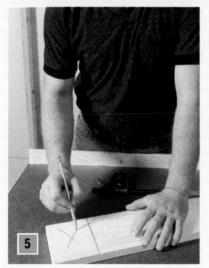

for the kerf by marking the waste side of the cutoff line with an X. This will help you avoid confusion as to side of the line on which to cut.

**6.** When cutting multiple pieces out of the same piece of lumber, make double marks to allow for the kerf.

# ■ Wood and Glue

Only when you're having trimwork specially milled will you need to be concerned about wood selection; otherwise you'll likely buy stock pieces and assemble them in your home to paint or stain. But if you're creating a new built-in bookcase, banquette, or fireplace mantel and surround, wood selection becomes important.

Wood is classified in two basic types: softwoods which come from coniferous trees and hardwoods wich come from deciduous trees.

Wood grades are based on the number of knots and the quality of the surface. Knots are only a cosmetic problem unless they are loose and likely to pop out. When selecting lumber, examine boards for the common problems of twist, bowing, cupping, crook, splits, and checking. A board with heavy twisting, bowing, cupping, or crooking is probably not useable. Splits on the end can be cut off; they will only get worse with time.

Checking, like knots, is most often just a cosmetic problem, see illustration below.

Lumber is sized using nominal dimensions, not actual dimensions. Nominal dimensions are slightly smaller. For example, a 2 x 4 is actually 1 ½ x 3 ½.

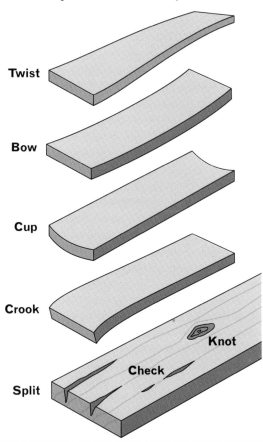

**Twist**

**Bow**

**Cup**

**Crook**

**Split**    **Check**    **Knot**

---

## TIPS AND TERMS

• Prices for any species of wood may vary greatly by region. Local woods are generally less expensive that species that have to be shipped a great distance.

• To save money, select wood based on the look of the grain and then stain to personal preferences. Cherry, for example, is an expensive wood but you can get the same look by buying birch and applying a cherry stain. The grain and hardness of cherry and birch are very similar.

• Hardwood lumber thickness is given in quarters of an inch. For example, a 2-inch thick piece of oak is called 8/4.

• Hardwood lumber is priced by the board foot. It's a volume measurement equal to 1 foot (width) by 1 foot (length) by 1 inch (thickness). A cherry board that's 6 inches wide, 1 inch (4/4) thick, and 4 feet long is equal to 4 board feet.

• It's always best to inspect lumber personally before buying. Every lumberyard has a lot of substandard boards in stock. If you call in an order, or if the lumberyard won't let you sort boards personally, be sure you can return boards you don't like after you've inspected them. Inspecting is also important to find the grain pattern you prefer and ensure all boards will have compatible grain patterns.

## COMMON WOOD GRADES

| Grade | Characteristic |
| --- | --- |
| Clear | No knots |
| Select or Select Structural | Very high-quality wood. Graded as 1,2,3 or A,B,C,D. The lower grades have more knots or blemishes. |
| No. 2 Common | Tight knots and few blemishes. A good choice for shelving. |
| No. 3 Common | Knots may be loose and surface may be blemished or damaged. |
| Construction or Standard | Good strength. Used for general framing |
| Utility | Used for rough framing |

**Since there is little stress on many trimwork joints, such as adding detail to a chair rail, a thin line of carpenter's glue may be all that's needed.**

### ADHESIVES

Many wood-working projects require an adhesive as well as nails or screws to hold pieces together. For general use, purchase a supply of wood glue; it's readily available at home centers and lumberyards. A hot-glue gun and glue sticks are suitable for small jobs that don't need much strength, such as holding a small piece of trim in place.

Construction adhesive in tubes and two-part epoxy for extra-strong holding are also commonly available but purchase those only if you need them for special applications. If you're installing wood paneling, look for a special paneling adhesive.

## SELECTING ADHESIVES

| Adhesive Type | Primary Use | Holding Power | Moisture Resistance | Set/Cure Time | Type of Applicator |
| --- | --- | --- | --- | --- | --- |
| Contact cement | Applying wood veneer and laminates | Excellent | Excellent | Must dry first/ 1-2 days | Brush or paint roller |
| Epoxy adhesive | Bonding almost any material | Excellent | Good | Must mix parts first/ 30 minutes to 10 hrs. | Throwaway brush or flat stick |
| Panel adhesive | Attaching paneling to walls | Good | Fair | 1 hour to 24 hours | Caulk tube or notched trowel |
| Carpenter's glue | Bonding wood pieces together | Good | Fair | 30 minutes to 24 hours | Squeeze-type container |
| Cyanoacrylate (superglue) | Bonding small items of almost any material | Good | Fair | 1 minute to 24 hours | Squeeze tube |

# ▮ Sanding

Working with wood always involves a few rough edges. Smooth those over with a good sanding before finishing a trimwork or built-in project. Any finish product, stain or paint, will not even out a surface. Applying those products to a rough surface will only serve to accentuate these surface flaws. Using the right tools and following a few tips makes the work go smoothly.

Getting a smooth surface is a progressive job. Plan on three separate sandings before paint or stain, and a sanding between each coat of finish. Start with an 80-grit sandpaper, then a 120-grit, and finally a 180- to 240-grit paper. Be sure to wipe the surface with a clean cloth between each sanding to remove all the dust.

Sanding is dusty work. Wear a dust mask. Seal off the work area to keep dust particles from spreading throughout the house.

Always use some type of sanding block, purchased or improvised, to get a uniform result and to minimize fatigue. Tear sandpaper to fit the block, or purchase sandpaper designed to fit the sanding block. Cutting sandpaper with scissors or a utility knife will dull the blade quickly. While sanding. regularly check the bottom of the block to make sure it is clean; debris can mar the surface and tear the sandpaper.

Always sand in the direction of the wood grain. Sanding across wood grain can leave scratches on the surface.

If you're using the right grade of sandpaper, you'll only need light strokes to get a uniform result.

To sand one surface without scratching the surface next to it, use masking tape to protect the adjoining surface that won't be sanded. Carefully affix the tape making sure it's adhering tightly all along the edge.

**A sanding block with a comfortable grip will make any sanding job easier. It's a good tool-box basic.**

**Smoothing the inside of a small opening requires just some sandpaper and your finger.**

**To remove excess wood putty and smooth the surface, very gently rub the surface with fine sandpaper.**

Sand carefully to avoid ripping the tape.

Sanding in tight spots requires a little ingenuity. You can buy a power detail sander for many applications. Sometimes, however, all you need is a small piece of scrap lumber—or even just your finger—to use as a sanding block. Simply wrap the sandpaper around the improvised sanding block and gently sand into corners and inside holes.

A power detail sander makes it easy to get into tight corners and around curves and get an even finish.

To get a crisp edge in tight places, wrap a piece of sandpaper around a small block of scrap wood.

When sanding newly applied trim, such as this simple chair rail, tape the edges to prevent damaging the adjoining wall. Use tape with a low-tack glue to avoid marring the wall surface.

Getting a consistent finish when sanding large areas with curves and angles requires a little backup. Use a dowel rod to anchor the sandpaper and make it easy to follow the contours.

# ■ Miter Cuts, Scribing, and The Compass

Strong, good-looking miter joints are essential to all carpentry and woodworking projects, while learning to scribe is a necessity for dealing with less-than-perfect walls. And anyone who has worked on even the most rudimentary carpentry projects will attest that driving nails is an important skill all its own.

## MAKING SIMPLE MITER CUTS

A *miter joint* is made when two pieces of wood are angle-cut or bevel-cut at the same angle then joined to form a corner. Most often two pieces that have been cut at 45 degrees are joined to make a 90-degree corner. *Miter cuts must be precise.* If they are off just one degree, the corner will be noticeably off.

The most cost-efficient way to make an angle cut is to use a miter box—essentially a jig for holding the saw at the proper angle to the work. Prior to placing the stock in the miter box, support it on a scrap of 1x4 or some other suitable material. This allows you to saw completely through the work without marring the bottom of the miter box. Place the member against the far side of the miter box, positioned as it will be when in use, and make the cut with a backsaw. Hold the work firmly against the back of the box with your free hand. If there's any secret to using a miter box effectively, it's in correctly measuring and marking for the cut rather than the cutting technique. If possible, make your miter cut first, then cut the other end of the piece to the proper length with a straight cut.

Achieving good miter cuts requires patience. Be sure to precisely mark the piece to be cut. Hold the piece firmly so it doesn't slide during cutting, and place the blade exactly on the cutting mark.

A good miter cut is preserved and enhanced by spending the time to line up mataching pieces and attaching them solidly. Use enough nails and glue to ensure a good fit.

If you're becoming a committed woodworker or plan to install a lot of trimwork, invest in a power miter saw. The accuracy and speed of cutting a power miter saw provides will greatly enhance the quality and speed of your projects, making the additional cost worthwhile.

## SCRIBING

Scribing is a simple technique that will allow you to fit moldings and cabinets to crooked walls. Using an inexpensive compass fitted with a sharp pencil you can transfer the profile of a wavy wall to your workpiece. Once the line is scribed, you need to file, plane or sand off the excess materials to create a nearly seamless fit.

**1.** Place the wood near the wall and parallel to it. Now, lock your compass at a setting that spans the gap, even at the widest point. Hold the compass at a consistent angle and draw it down the wall, marking the board. In this case, the edge of the compass, not its point, rides along the wall.

**2.** Securely clamp the scribed board to your worktable, then sand the scribed line. Using a coarse belt, tilt your sander backward to undercut the line for a snug fit against the wall. If there's a lot of stock to remove, cut with a jigsaw just to the waste side of the line, removing the bulk of material before sanding.

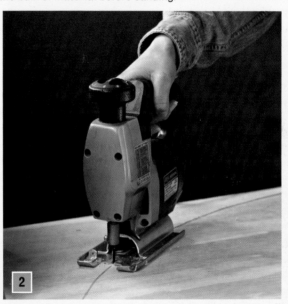

## THE COMPASS

This little gem from grammar school geometry is a great addition to your tool box. Keep a compass handy for many situations. For example, cutting away just the right amount for a door to clear a threshold or following the contours of a wall so a kitchen backsplash or countertop fits perfectly.

Use a compass to find the center of a board by opening it just wider than half the width. Mark two half circles. The intersection points marks the midpoint.

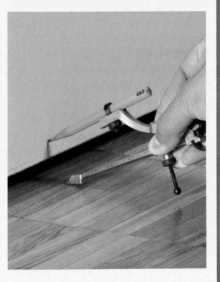

# ■ Nailing and Setting Screws

Properly setting nails and screws on trimwork, cabinets, and built-ins will give your work a polished look. The goal is to make these pieces almost invisible.

1. To nail two pieces together, first mark where the nail will go with an awl or the tip of the nail. This divot helps ensure that the nail won't accidentally move from it's place when you hammer it hard enough to break the wood's surface.

2. With thumb and forefinger, hold the nail vertically and grip the hammer near the end of the handle. Lightly tap the nail until it stands by itself. Once the nail is set, remove your hand. Keep your eye on the nail as you swing the hammer. Relax and let your whole arm move, swinging from the shoulder. Keep your wrist loose so you can give the hammer a snap at the end of each blow.

3. Stop swinging when the nail head is flush or nearly flush with the surface of the wood.

4. For exposed applications, such as the trim around a window, use a nail set to gently sink the small head of the finish nail to just below the surface. Fill with wood putty to cover the hole.

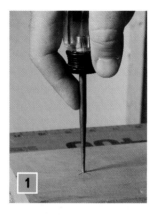

## CLEANING THE BIT

Drilling through several pieces of wood can clog a drill bit, especially if you're drilling a lot of holes.

**1.** If the drill starts to bind, don't force it further. Instead, feed the drill bit slowly into the wood, backing it out frequently while the motor is running. This pulls trapped wood particles back to the surface.

**2.** Wet or sappy wood may clog the bit even if you're proceeding slowly. If this happens, stop drilling and use the tip of a nail to scrape out the wood particles. If the bit jams, reverse the drill rotation and be sure to pull the bit straight out.

## SETTING SCREWS

Setting screws properly requires drilling three holes.
**1.** The first hole, the pilot hole, is drilled through both pieces using a bit that is slightly smaller than the shank of the screw.
**2.** Next, enlarge the hole using a bit that is as thick as the screw change.

**3.** To ensure that the head of the screw will sit flush with or slightly below the surface of the wood, use a countersink bit.
**4.** The screw should slide easily through the top countersink hole, gripping tightly as it passes to the smaller hole.

For driving a large number of screws, buy a combination countersink-counterbore bit. It does the three prep steps in one.

# Squaring, Plumbing, and Leveling

Many trimwork projects like shelving and cabinets require that you *square* your work which means making sure one surface is at a 90-degree angle to another. It's important to check for square at every stage of your work: corners, uprights and board ends.

Having work be *plumb* (perpendicular to the earth) and *level* (parallel to the earth) is equally important. Don't assume existing walls or floors are square, level or plumb. Most often they are not due to imperfect construction or settling that has taken place over years. Learning techniques to check these things will keep your trimwork projects straight and true.

## CHECKING FOR SQUARE

**1.** All your careful measuring will be wasted if you start with a piece of lumber that is not square—one edge will be longer than the other. Check the board end by holding a combination square with the body or handle firmly against a factory edge. If the end isn't square, mark a line and trim the board.

**2.** You can also use a combination square to check for either 45- or 90-degree angles. Also, by sliding the blade, you can check depths. A word of caution—if this tool is dropped it can go out of square, so check it once in a while against a square factory edge like a sheet of plywood.

**3.** For larger jobs, use a framing square. Lay the square up against two members where they meet. If the tongue and the blade of the square rest neatly against the members, the sides are square. Or place the square on the outside. Again, if the square touches the members at all points, the unit is square.

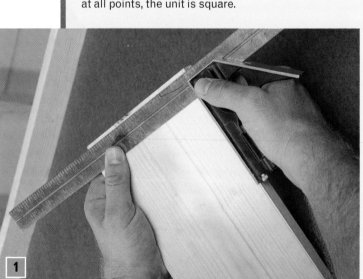

## CHECKING FOR PLUMB AND LEVEL

**1.** To see if a piece is plumb (perfectly vertical), hold a level against one face of the vertical surface and look at the bubble in the level's lower glass vial. If it rests between the two guide marks, the piece is plumb.

**2.** If you're installing cabinets it's important to make sure they are plumb in both directions or the doors will shut or open by themselves. With the cabinet fastened loosely to the wall, hold a level against a vertical framing piece. Tap in shims until the bubble indicates the cabinet is plumb.

In most cases, you can simply place your carpenter's level on a piece to see if it's level. Raise or lower the piece until the bubble rests between the marks, mark the position of the piece and remove the level (you don't want to risk your level getting knocked to the floor).

**3.** In a tight spot, use the smaller level that comes on some combination squares or a torpedo level, a shorter version of the carpenter's level.

Or, if you already know that an adjoining member of wall is plumb, check that the piece is square to it.

# ■ Filling and Finishing

Paint, stain and clear finishes rarely cover up imperfections in wood. Often they make things look worse rather than better. It pays to prepare your wood carefully before you add a finish.

Fill in holes with wood filler and sand the surface smooth. If you're applying a clear finish, limit your use of putty to small spots; even putty made to accept stain never looks like real wood. Even if you plan to paint the surface, cover exposed plywood edges. They soak up paint like a sponge and will look rough no matter how many coats of paint you apply.

Once the wood surface is prepared, match your paint, stain, or clear finish to the intended use of your project.

## FILLING HOLES

**1.** For small nail and screw holes, use a dough-type wood filler. Apply filler either before or after staining; experiment to find out which looks best. Begin by tamping a small amount of the filler into the hole with your thumb. Smooth it with a putty knife. Wipe away the excess with a rag dampened with water or mineral spirits depending on the type of putty (check manufacturer's directions).

**2.** To conceal a plywood edge, cut a thin piece of molding to fit, apply carpenter's glue to the edge, and fasten the molding with brads (small finishing screws).

**3.** You can also cover an edge with wood veneer tape. Buy tape that is wider than the thickness of the material and that matches its surface. Cut the tape with scissors allowing at least ¼ inch extra on all edges. Position iron-on tape carefully so it covers the edge along the entire length. Apply even, steady pressure with a household iron set on high. Trim the edges with a sharp knife, then lightly sand the corners.

**4.** If you need to paint the entire surface of a project, water-mix putty excels at filling shallow depressions over a large surface area. The putty sets up quickly, so don't mix more than you can use in 10 minutes. To fill cracks around a knot, mix the putty to a pastelike consistency and force it into all the cracks with a putty knife. Feather out the patch to the surrounding wood.

**5.** To fill the edges of plywood or the end grain of boards, mix the putty to a thinner consistency. Sand and apply a second coat if necessary. For deep holes, you may have to apply two layers to allow for any shrinkage of the first layer of putty.

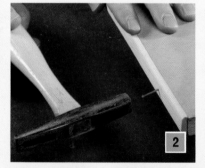
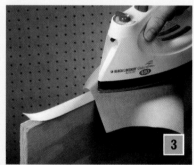

# FINISHING TECHNIQUES

Brushing on paint and stain require two different application techniques for best results.

### Painting Correctly

**1.** Painting with a brush may seem like a simple task, but keep these tips in mind. Apply paint to wood surfaces with short strokes across the wood grain, laying down paint in both directions. Don't bear down too hard on the bristles.

**2.** Finish painting with longer strokes in one direction only—going with the wood grain. Use just the tips of the bristles to smooth out the paint.

### Applying Stain

**1.** Apply stain with a brush and wait a few minutes. The heavier the application and the longer you wait, the deeper the color.

**2.** Wipe with a clean rag, taking care to make the color even throughout the piece. To make it darker, apply a second coat. If it is too dark, rub with a cloth moistened with the recommended paint thinner.

# Glossary

**Apron.** The board that rests under the sill.

**Backsaw.** A straight fine-toothed saw often used with a miter box to create clean-edged miter cuts for trimwork.

**Balusters.** The vertical support in a staircase design commonly formed from square or tapered spindles and slats placed closely together.

**Balustrade.** This refers to the entire staircase railing including the top handrail and the individual spindles or balusters.

**Banquette.** A popular style of window seat most often used as seating in a breakfast nook or dining area.

**Baseboard.** A trimboard attached as part of a base treatment to the bottom of a wall where the wall meets the floor.

**Bay window.** Combinations of three or more windows projecting outward from a room usually made up of a larger center unit and two flanking units at 30-, 45-, or 90-degree angles to the wall.

**Bevel cut.** A cut made at an angle through the thick dimension of a piece of wood.

**Bracket.** A support—real or decorative—used beneath shelving, cabinets or a fireplace mantel.

**Bow window.** A variation on the bay window, bow windows are made up of four or more window units joined together at equal angles to form a curve.

**Box beam.** A ceiling decoration involving a bottom face board joined at its edges by two side boards to form a basic box. The form is repeated across the ceiling.

**Butt joint.** A joint formed by two pieces of material when fastened end to end, end to face, or end to edge.

**Casing.** Molding around a door, window, or other opening.

**Chair rail.** A horizontal band of trim installed on a wall between the floor and the ceiling. Usually placed about 3 feet above the floor.

**Chalk line.** A marking tool filled with colored chalk used to mark long straight lines.

**Clamshell casing.** The name for the plain, slightly curved trim used in many builder homes.

**Coffered ceiling.** Set with square or polygonal panels, this decorative treatment combines solid or hardwood beams with molding to form a grid. The ceiling itself can be left plain or painted or paneled.

**Column.** A vertical support member, typically with a cylindrical or square shaft that can be structural, decorative or both. They are used to support a beam or ceiling, frame a passageway or create an open room divider.

**Corbel.** A carved block or bracket projecting from a wall used to support a beam or other horizontal member.

**Cornice.** A molding or group of moldings used in the corner between a wall and a ceiling.

**Crown molding.** A single piece of molding that installs at an angle to its adjoining surfaces. Typically used to decorate the intersection between a wall and ceiling or to top a cabinet or built in.

**Decorative cornice.** A custom box shaped design that adds a decorative topping to a window treatment while providing a place to conceal curtain rods or other window treatment apparatus.

**Dentil.** A series of decorative small projecting squares or "teeth" that often adorn a cornice or other interior molding.

**Door casing.** Trim that surrounds the edges of a door frame.

**Entablature.** In classical architecture, the horizontal assembly supported by columns or other structures and consisting of an architrave, frieze, and cornice. On a fireplace, it refers to the upper horizontal section of the mantel that joins together the pilasters.

**Field.** The inverted "U" frame that defines the shape of a fireplace mantel.

**Frieze.** Part of the entablature, a typically flat molding that could have a decorative relief carving or classical profile.

**Header.** The framing component spanning a door or window opening in a wall.

**Jamb.** The top and side frames of a door or window opening.

**Joist.** Horizontal framing members that support a floor and/or ceiling.

**Level.** The condition that exists when a surface is true horizontal. Also the name of the tool used to determine that a surface is level.

**Mantel.** The entire decorative surround of a fireplace.

**Medallion.** A decorative, usually round relief carving applied to a wall or ceiling.

**Miter joint.** The joint formed when two members meet that have been cut at the same angle, usually 45 degrees.

**Molding.** A decorative strip of wood or plastic, usually small-dimensioned, used in various kinds of trimwork.

**Muntins.** The dividers between panes of glass. Also referred to as mullions.

**Nail set.** A blunt-pointed metal tool used to sink the heads of finishing nails below the surface of the wood.

**Newell post.** The starting point of a staircase design, it can be square, cylindrical or some other custom shape. It is traditional to embellish them with recesses and other trim features.

**Niche.** A decorative display area, usually recessed into the wall that is defined by its gently sloping sides.

**Nook.** Similar to a niche, this decorative display area features sides that are squared off.

**Palladian window.** A large arced window inspired by the classical style of Italian Renaissance architect Andrea Palladio.

**Panel.** Sometimes used interchangeably with wainscot, full height wall treatments are always referred to as paneling.

**Picture rail.** A decorative strip that features wires hooked over the molding, extended down the wall and attached to the back of a framed photo or painting.

**Pilaster.** A shallow, square-edged column that has the appearance of a full-sized column that has been embedded into a wall with only it's front side visible.

**Pilot hole.** A small hole drilled into a wooden member to avoid splitting the wood when driving in a screw or a nail.

**Plate rail.** A decorative feature that involves a wide molding strip designed to display plates and picture frames.

**Plinth.** A rectangular block that serves as the base of a vertical door casing or pilaster.

**Plumb.** The condition that exists when a member is at true vertical.

**Riser.** The vertical element that combines with a tread to form a step.

**Rosette.** A decorative corner block used to join the head and side casings around a door.

**Scarf joint.** The connection between two pieces of trim joined by overlapping opposing miters in order to disguise the joint.

**Shim.** A thin strip or wedge of wood or other material used to fill a gap between two adjoining components or to help establish level or plumb.

**Sill.** The horizontal surface installed below the sash of a window sometimes referred to as a window stool.

**Soffit.** A built in structure that projects down from a ceiling. Often used to conceal utility lines and structural beams they can also be decorative elements that give a ceiling a custom look.

**Square.** The condition that exists when one surface is at a 90-degree angle to another. Also a tool used to determine square.

**Studs.** Vertical wood or metal framing members spaced at regular intervals within a wall.

**Transom.** A window above a door—it can have moving parts for opening or be fixed.

**Tread.** The horizontal part of a stair you step on.

**Veneer.** A thin layer of wood, often a decorative wood laminated to the surface of a more common wood.

**Wainscot.** A decorative finish along the lower portion of a wall.

**Window casing.** Trim that surrounds the edges of a window frame.

**Window stool.** The horizontal surface installed below the sash of a window, often referred to as a windowsill.

# ■ Index

# Transform your home

## into the living space you've always wanted

DISCARD

STANLEY **COMPLETE**

ALL NEW EDITION

new **decorati** bo

**Trimw** & Carpentry

STANLEY **COMPLETE**

**Built-In** Shelves & Bookca

Better Homes and Gardens

**colo** scheme made

Better Homes and Gardens

decorative **paint** techniques & ideas

*Imagine* living in a space customized for you, by you. These great titles will help make your dreams come true with style ideas, design tips and step-by-step instructions.

**M**eredith BOOKS

ADT0249_0407